The Revd Dr Emma Percy is Chaplain a
College, Oxford. She was among the fi
ordained priest in the Church of Engl:
selected as a deaconess and ordained as a deacon. She has experience
of both parish and chaplaincy ministry, including seven years as a
vicar in Millhouses, Sheffield. She is married to a priest and together
they have brought up two boys who are now flying the nest. Emma's
research interests are in the ministry of the Church of England and
the theology of mothering. She was awarded a PhD from the University
of Nottingham for her work in this area, which is published as
Mothering as a Metaphor for Ministry (Ashgate, 2014). She has spoken
at conferences and workshops for clergy in many different contexts.
She does much of her thinking while walking her bearded collie and
relaxes by doing yoga, reading novels and baking biscuits.

WHAT CLERGY DO

Especially when it looks like nothing

Emma Percy

First published in Great Britain in 2014

Society for Promoting Christian Knowledge
36 Causton Street
London SW1P 4ST
www.spckpublishing.co.uk

Copyright © Emma Percy 2014

British Library Cataloguing-in-Publication Data
A catalogue record for this book is available from the British Library

ISBN 978–0–281–07024–4
eBook ISBN 978–0–281–07025–1

Typeset by Graphicraft Limited, Hong Kong
First printed in Great Britain by Ashford Colour Press
Subsequently digitally printed in Great Britain

eBook by Graphicraft Limited, Hong Kong

Produced on paper from sustainable forests

To the people of Holy Trinity, Millhouses, Sheffield,
with thanks for all we did together

Contents

Introduction

This is a book about parish ministry. I am writing it because I know that there is a lot of good parish ministry going on. There are many good enough parish priests working hard with and for people in a wide variety of parish situations. These priests sustain people through the trials of life, while encouraging growth and maturity of faith in all those they care for. This book aims to encourage them in their ministry and to give them, perhaps, some richer language to affirm what they are doing. The book draws parallels between the role of a mother and that of a parish priest. I will explain why I think that this is a helpful metaphor to envision the caring relationship and activity that is parish ministry. It will allow me to explore the doing of ministry with terms such as 'comforting' and 'cherishing', learning from the process of weaning, housekeeping and other maternal practices. In this book I am attempting to find ways to talk about and value the ordinary day-to-day stuff of parish ministry. I do this through discussing not the tasks clergy do but the attitudes and ways of thinking and acting which characterize good parish ministry.

On being asked what his father did a young child responded with, 'Oh, he is very busy being kind to sad old ladies.' This young boy was aware that his father did not go out to an office somewhere each morning as others did but frequently left home at random times of day because someone needed to see him; someone was sad and his father had a role in supporting him. His dad was a parish priest living and working out of a vicarage next door to the church. It is not surprising that a small boy can only grasp one aspect of his father's job. However, one of the complex and frustrating realities for a parish priest is that it seems many people are not quite sure what it is that they do. People are conscious of the services, and many vicars smile politely when greeted with, 'Sunday's your busy day' or 'Christmas is the busy time of year'. Most parish clergy work long hours, and yet they can still feel that they are only scratching the surface of all they should be doing. Those who are in stipendiary

1

posts live and work on the job, creating difficulty at times in drawing neat lines between being on or off duty. A vicar wearing a dog collar or robed for a service is easily recognizable, but beyond the idea that he or she is a professional church worker, do people have an understanding of what a parish priest does day to day?

There have been many books published about being a priest or being in church leadership which set out to answer this question, so why add another to the mix? I am writing this because many of the books I have read about being a priest leave me feeling guilty or exhausted. Some quite appropriately focus on the spirituality of priesthood but can end up suggesting that clergy have to be the most prayerful and most spiritual people in a church. I know that I am not and am unlikely to be. Clearly, ordination brings with it the responsibility to maintain and develop a robust spiritual life. However, ordination does not make clergy more holy or more prayerful than other Christians. Most ministry is sustained by the prayerful spirituality of faithful members of the congregation. The books that make me feel exhausted are those which seem to suggest that the vicar has to do everything. Such books often fail to provide a way of integrating all the busyness into a reasonable life.

Another problem is that some writers, in order to affirm that priests work in different spheres of ministry, end up offering a rather general picture of ordained ministry without grounding it in the particularity of parish life or other contexts. I have worked in both parish and sector ministry. I am a priest in both, but how that is worked out is different. As a chaplain in the world of higher education, I work in and for a community which has as its primary focus education and research. I bring the Christian faith into conversation with the community but it does not shape its purpose. A parish priest has responsibility for an organization that has the primary purpose of living out and witnessing to the truths of the Christian faith. In both worlds there are similarities in the way priests work but there are also important differences in the responsibilities held and the relationships of shared collaborative ministry present. Therefore this book is focusing on the relationship and activity of a parish priest. It envisions an incumbent with a parish. I am aware that many clergy are caring simultaneously for a number of parishes and I hope they can imaginatively stretch the metaphors to encompass a bigger family.

However, the biggest issue is that in writing about parish ministry there seems to be a lack of good language. That is, there is a lack of imagery which resonates with life experience and helps to express what it is that clergy do. Biblical writing is full of imagery and metaphor. Jesus' parables draw on everyday examples – stewards, agricultural labourers, shepherds and even a housewife. Paul talks about those in ministry as servants, builders and farmers. He also on occasions uses the imagery of father, and perhaps more surprisingly mother, to talk about his care for the Christian communities he worked with. There seems to be a dearth of good metaphors in current writing about ministry. There are traditional images such as a priest being like a shepherd. Yet most of us have little experience of actual shepherding so cannot pick up on the resonances and insights the metaphor was intended to offer. There is a renewed emphasis on the imagery of servant for ministry but, as I will discuss later in the book, the language of servant for those engaged in service industries has been dropped in our culture. Thus when we talk about servant leadership there is little experience of the kind of system of servants and slaves which was commonplace to previous generations. This means that the term is often used more like an adjective than a noun.

My suggestion is to take an image which we see all around us. This image is of a mother caring for her children. We all have some experience of this and many of us have intense hands-on practice of it. It is not a totally new image for thinking about ministry but it is not a common one.[1] There are plenty of ways in which parish ministry is like mothering. In saying this I am not suggesting that priests should be female, or that those women who are mothers make better priests. Men and women, those who have or have not brought up children, can all learn from reflecting on mothering. I have had the opportunity of sharing some of the ideas in this book with a wide variety of ordinands and clergy. The fact that those who were not mothers found the ideas helpful, as well as those who were, was one of the motivations for writing.

Like mothering, the role of a parish priest does not fit into many of the modern ideas about work and professionalism. It is a commitment that does not lend itself to targets and easily measurable outcomes. Neither role can be done by formula; there is not a definitive right way to do it but lots of shared wisdom, which can help. Naomi Stadlen wrote a wonderful book about the early years of mothering called *What Mothers Do: Especially when it looks like nothing.*[2] Her aim was to try to articulate the valuable and meaningful activity of mothering, which is so often dismissed. A tired mother can get to the end of the day and say, 'I got nothing done', when she has in fact been actively caring for her baby all day. In a world of productivity and tangible outcomes this kind of hard work is in danger of going unremarked.

Parish clergy can also find it hard to find the right words to describe all the busyness of sustaining church life. It is easy to make lists of services taken, funerals conducted and meetings chaired, but how do we begin to talk about the time and energy expended on caring for all the different people in the parish? Are the times spent drinking coffee with Maureen, listening to Ted's take on the world, singing nursery rhymes with the toddlers and catching up in the supermarket with Jane's latest health scare, really work? Even with something more concrete, like a funeral, how do we begin to quantify and describe all the attentive energy needed to support these people through the loss of a loved one, to deliver a meaningful service within the tight time limit of the crematorium chapel and to chat meaningfully to all sorts of strangers afterwards?

In order to help us think and talk about this I draw parallels between the role of a parish priest and that of a mother. As well as drawing on Stadlen's work, I use ideas on mothering developed by Sara Ruddick in *Maternal Thinking*[3] and unpick the concept of an 'ordinary good enough mother' coined by the paediatrician Donald Winnicott. Being 'good enough' does not mean being mediocre or simply satisfactory. It is a term which acknowledges the relational nature of the role and the complexity of all the demands. A good enough mother is one who responds appropriately to her child often enough for him to feel safe and secure but not in a way that smothers him. He needs to learn to do some things for himself if he is to mature. Thus mothers hold close and let go, learning through the practice the necessary wisdom to know when to do which.

This is not an exhaustive book about all aspects of parish ministry. It does not provide answers or offer 'how to' advice. My hope is that it will become a conversation partner for those reflecting on their ministry. By expressing things in a different language and by suggesting different metaphors, I aim to enrich the conversation. I hope that some of the parallels I draw between mothering and ministry will provide moments of epiphany enabling fresh ways of seeing things. I hope that this will inspire those in ministry to feel more comfortable about expressing their own metaphors, drawing on other life experiences to help articulate the work they are doing. Above all I hope that this will help us all to champion the less remarkable aspects of the day-to-day life of building up communities of faith, where God is worshipped and people are both cherished and encouraged to grow. I write out of my own experience, so I use a feminine pronoun for a priest and masculine pronoun for a child. These could easily be reversed.

1

A priest-in-charge

———•◆•———

When I moved to Sheffield to the parish of Holy Trinity, Millhouses, the living had been suspended so I was initially licensed as priest-in-charge. This was my first incumbency and I found myself reflecting on what it meant to be in charge. One way of interpreting the terminology is to see the priest-in-charge as the boss. Priests are in charge in the sense that they are running the organization, they have the final say on how things are done and the buck stops with them. However, I was uncomfortable with the idea of being the boss. I needed to reflect on whether this was simply because I was nervous about the responsibility or whether there was another way to understand the role. If I was the boss, how did I relate my role to the collective ministry of the church? If I shared the current understanding of collaborative ministry, could I find a better way of expressing what it meant for me to be in charge?

In this chapter I will reflect on these questions. First, I will look at the issues around understanding a parish priest as a professional. It is a profession but not quite like other professions. The language of leadership is often used to discuss the role of a parish priest. Yet this can be problematic as the term needs qualifying to be meaningful. So, second, I will discuss the ambiguity of leadership language and of the popular term 'servant leader'. If being in charge cannot simply be equated with being the leader, how should it be understood? It can mean being responsible for someone or something, and the latter part of the chapter will explore this way of understanding charge, relating it to care. Third, I will suggest that, as an image of responsible caring, mothering can provide a rich metaphor for thinking about ministry. As with all metaphors, this is about drawing on the resonances around one image to enhance our understanding of something else.

Parish priests – a profession

In the past, clergy in the Church of England were simply educated men who took on a role with a social status and related duties. Anglican clergy were not trained specifically for their work as vicars, rectors or curates. A good education or a well-connected family was considered good enough preparation. The idea of actually training people for the work of a parish ministry developed in the Church of England in the nineteenth century alongside a growing concept of professionalism in many other areas of work. Anthony Russell, in *The Clerical Profession*, outlines this shift in the self-identity of clergy as they developed through the nineteenth century alongside other professions.[1] The concept of theological colleges was to some extent motivated by the opening up of university education to members of other Christian denominations. The college at Cuddesdon, founded in 1855, is a good example. It was initially a kind of Anglican finishing school for postgraduate men.

Russell points out that, although the concept of a clerical profession developed alongside ideas about professionalism in law, teaching and other areas, this is a profession that is not quite like other professions. The skill set of clergy is not clearly defined in the way it is with lawyers, doctors or teachers. This is still true in today's Church. Clergy are professionally trained but they then enter a profession which is rather flat, lacking the kind of progression present in other walks of life. The structured systems of promotion, pay scales and increasing responsibility present in many professions are not part of the experience of most clergy.

A priest may arrive at a parish to be in charge after anything from 3 to 30 years of parish experience and the role will be the same, with the same stipend. This is still an issue for clergy self-identity. There is also a problem about defining and describing the professional skills particular to the work of clergy. Ministry division has moved to a language of competencies which should be applicable to clergy, but inevitably the terminology is open to interpretation and not neatly quantifiable. This can lead to rather general statements about leadership ability and spiritual depth, which require discernment to judge rather than any easily demonstrated skills. Priests are ordained after a process of discerning their character rather than measuring specific skills. Clergy are trained, but this is as much about forming a character as about acquiring knowledge. As Martyn Percy maintains in *Clergy: The Origin of Species*, Anglican clergy can only ever be partly professional.[2]

A parish needs a priest

Alongside questions of professional identity are issues around the theology of ordination. The opening up of university to people of different theological traditions, mentioned above, sharpened questions about Anglican orders. The Oxford Movement in the mid-nineteenth century, which sought to reaffirm the catholicity of the Church of England, stressed the continuity of Anglican orders, the importance of Apostolic Succession and the distinctive nature of those ordained. This catholic theology of ordination is still an important strand of Anglicanism. Yet many Anglicans have a far more functional understanding of ordination shaped by protestant theology and the traditions of reformed churches, with less distinction between the ministry of lay and ordained.

Increasingly in the late twentieth century, ecumenical discussions emphasized the priesthood of all believers. This has led to an increased expectation of the ministry of all and a growth in formally licensed lay ministries. Yet the reality of how the laity engages in ministry, formally and informally, is still contested. The Church of England continues to maintain the distinctive nature of ordination, and yet what that distinction is, and its significance, are not clearly defined.

The distinctive role of the ordained may be understood as ontological; priests are simply different because they are ordained. On the other hand, it might be purely functional; this is a job they do. Usually it is a complex mixture of the two, assumed rather than properly articulated. The distinction is often talked about as if we all know what it is. I recently spotted an advertisement for an archdeacon which required the candidate to be able to 'relate to both lay and ordained' as if they were two different species![3] There are authorized lay and ordained ministries, but apart from certain sacramental and legal responsibilities it is not very clear how they actually differ. There is a sense in which people know they are different, but how to explain that succinctly is difficult. Despite these problems of definition, it is accepted that a parish church requires a priest, and to be licensed in charge of a parish, to be an incumbent, it is necessary to be ordained.

At a basic level this is because a priest is able to provide the necessities of church life. That is, a priest is able to preside at the sacraments which sustain the life of the faithful. This is true whether the theology explains this as an outcome of an ontological change consequent to ordination or as a point of order and authority within the life of the Church of England. When a priest is not in charge, when there is a vacancy, then other priests need to be found to enable the sacraments to be celebrated. Some priests may preside at the sacraments in ways that we find more aesthetically pleasing than others, more in tune with our understanding of worship, more audibly or more engagingly, but Anglican theology is clear that those things make no actual difference to the reality of the sacraments.[4] They may well affect how we feel about the experience of worship but someone has still been baptized, we have been absolved and have received the body and blood of Christ, because a priest has carried out his or her role in accordance with the authorized liturgies of the Church.

There are, of course, continuing debates on who can be a priest in the Church of England in terms of gender. And I am aware that some are uncomfortable with terms like 'sacrament' or 'priest', preferring a more functional theology of church order. Yet the tradition and practice of the Church is to ordain men, and now women, as priests/presbyters and to accept that it is because they are ordained that they play a necessary part in the validity of the sacraments, which are a means by which God's grace is manifest in the life of the Church. Our accepted church theology makes this distinction between the lay and the ordained. So a church community needs access to a priest

A church leader?

When this priest is in charge as rector or vicar or simply licensed as in charge, it is assumed that this conveys more than the role of presiding at the sacraments. That aspect of the priest's role is a given but her responsibility is wider. It has become increasingly common to describe this wider aspect of a parish priest's role as church leadership. Yet 'leadership' is in essence a rather vague term. In order for it to make sense there needs to be some explanation of who or what is being led, and to where. For instance, it is possible to talk meaningfully about those who lead worship in church. There are clear structures about who is leading, who is being led. There is also a clearly defined purpose, to create a coherent worshipping experience where the congregation can suitably offer their praise and prayers to God. This is an area where clergy are leaders. Yet so are other people; other clergy, lay ministers, musicians and talented laity all play their part in leading worship appropriately.

However, when we talk about church leadership the implication is something more than the specific tasks of leading a service; it is about the planning, strategizing and implementing of what it means to be the Church in that place. There is an underlying assumption that the vicar, as well as playing a significant role in leading the worship and a primary role in the sacramental aspects of such worship, is also in some way overseeing, shaping and actualizing the ministry that is the purpose of the church. So the general catch-all term of 'church leader' is offered as a way of defining what a vicar does.

The term 'leader', though, does not necessarily help in defining what this wider role consists of. A priest may well be in charge, but not quite in the way leadership works in other professions. Just as clergy do not experience the kinds of pay scales and career structures that are part of other professions, they also find themselves in charge of communities which do not have the kinds of clear structures that most organizations have. A parish priest does not have the same kind of job definitions or clear parameters as the CEO of a business or the head teacher of a school. Parish churches are run for the most part by volunteers, so structures are not shaped by employment, pay, contracts and productivity. Power is therefore ambiguous and at times contested. Martyn Percy writes;

> Part of the difficulty for most clergy is that, unlike the conductor of an orchestra, or the CEO of a major corporation, they lack the powerbase to execute decisive initiatives or decisions . . . There is no relationship of compulsion between the leader of the church and the led.[5]

That last statement is an important point; the relationship between the one in charge and those who make up a church congregation is complex. A priest may have a clear sense of what she wants to happen but cannot compel others to do as she says or 'sack' those who do not. It is also not easy to define the work the church is engaged in. We may have begun to devise pithy statements to define our ministry in a given place. Yet unlike other businesses, there are no tangible products and not even easily measurable outcomes.

The Ordinal, the service in which priests are ordained, outlines the diversity of the Church's work. It is to offer worship to God, to be the community in which people develop as disciples of Christ, growing up in faith – a community marked by mutual love and service. The local church is to care for those beyond the gathered community and it is to be a community of witness, proclaiming the good news of Christ that others might come to believe. Such things do not lend themselves to easily definable strategies and measurable targets. For all of this to happen, the whole church community needs to be involved. All have responsibilities for their own discipleship as well as their witness, mutual love and service.

In the New Testament, Paul offers the image of a body, in which all parts are necessary, as a metaphor for the Church. The head of this body is not a human leader but Christ, whom all members are seeking to follow. Within the body there are those gifted in ways that can help the whole community develop: teaching, evangelism, service, apostleship. It is presumed that those who have such gifts will utilize them for building up the community. They are not confined to the ordained, but there is an expectation that a priest, who is in charge of a parish, will exhibit some of these gifts and use them to sustain and direct the church community. Yet as noted above, this priest does not have a clearly defined position from which to compel the rest of the community to follow her lead. Martyn Percy maintains that:

> Clergy very seldom have the privilege of being strategic; they only have the possibility of being tactical and pragmatic. Moreover, even when they think they are being strategic in leadership, no assumptions can be made about the tactics and pragmatism of the laity in the congregation.[6]

Thus to understand being in charge as being the leader requires the humility to acknowledge the ambiguity of a priest's authority and the acceptance that the ministry of the church is always collective. In fact, clergy are leading a community within which others hold defined leadership roles and still others undefined ones which may carry a lot of weight. Defined roles in a given parish may include other clergy, who share the authority that comes with ordination; authorized lay ministers; churchwardens with legal responsibilities for the buildings and proper ordering of services; the PCC, elected and also having legal responsibilities; and directors of music and others who lead aspects of worship.

Yet these recognized leaders in a given church are still only a part of the collective ministry of the whole community. The informal authority of individuals within a congregation can have an immense impact on the life and witness of a given church. Individuals who have a long history with a certain place can wield immense authority. They may thwart strategies for change or positively motivate others by their support for them. The integrity of individuals within a church congregation can impact on whether others from the community trust, or do not trust, the message the church proclaims. A well-phrased mission statement and coherent plan of action can be derailed by individuals who are unwelcoming to newcomers. A lack of pastoral care for the marginalized in a congregation may undermine the assertion that the church witnesses to the love of God. Clergy can and should inspire, motivate and encourage the whole community in their discipleship and ministry but, as Martyn Percy says, they cannot compel. The health of the ministry of a given church requires, as Paul's body metaphor reminds us, the working together of all its parts.

Servant leadership

It therefore follows that the concept of the priest-in-charge as the leader needs to be qualified to acknowledge that this leadership is not akin to being the boss, or an organizational head, with clear chains of command and an agreed product. One way of qualifying the term, which seems to be currently popular, is to talk about 'servant leadership'. The priest is a leader but also a servant, combining the sense of responsibility of the leader with the orientation of a servant. It draws on New Testament language of *diakonia*: ministry as service. Yet servant, like leader, is a concept in need of further definition.

To be a servant for someone or some institution is to do things for them that free them up to do and be whatever their primary task is. I currently work in an Oxford college, and until recently all non-academic staff were called college servants. This ranged from those who cleaned rooms to the accountant and librarian. They were servants, not because they did lowly tasks but because they did necessary tasks which freed the academics to focus on studying and teaching; each role had specific areas of responsibility. This sense of role responsibilities is important because in order to be a good servant the actual tasks that fall to you need to be agreed. We only have to watch the television programme *Downton Abbey* to understand how the role of servants is defined and stratified. The difference between a footman and a valet is vitally important, as is the great gulf between a kitchen maid and a lady's maid. 'Servant' is not an adjective but a noun, and just as a leader needs to have an understanding of what and who is being led where, so a servant needs to know what tasks fall to his or her area of responsibility.

There is an important sense in which clergy are servants ministering to the congregation, setting them free to focus on their primary task of living out their Christian discipleship in the world, and I will explore this further in a later chapter. Yet too often the term 'servant' is simply used like an adjective to imply an attitude and to counter concerns about leadership. It leaves unanswered important questions. Whose servant is the priest? The congregation's, the bishop's? All Christians are servants of Christ: how is the priest's servanthood distinctive? Is the priest a senior civil servant, the top of a hierarchy of servants and, if so, how does she relate to those who are also servants but in far more menial positions? The use of the term 'servant' does not remove hierarchical ideas even though the intention is often to counteract authoritarian models of leadership. There is a danger that the term leaves priests torn between being the boss and being the servant who must meet all needs. Many clergy struggle as they try to be both.

In charge – being responsible for

If we go back to the terminology of priest-in-charge, I suggest that we can look for a different way of interpreting the phrase and in doing so begin to find different ways to think and talk about the role of parish clergy. Instead of seeing 'in charge' as being the boss or the leader, we can think about how having charge of someone or something can be understood as having a responsibility to care for them. As a child I sometimes travelled on my own on the train in the charge of the guard. That meant that the guard kept a kindly eye on me, made sure I got off at the right station with all my belongings and that someone was there to meet me. Clearly, if there had been a difficult incident on the train or if I had become ill or distressed he would have had to become more involved, but usually he played his part in the smooth running of the train service and occasionally checked that I was doing OK. This understanding of 'charge' relates to a sense of oversight and care. Those who cared for children as nannies and nursemaids often referred to them as their charges. It conveys both responsibility and care.

There is nothing original about suggesting that care is a central component of the role of a parish priest. The pastoral side of ministry has long been connected to images of care, but I do think that it is important in our modern culture to reaffirm the centrality of care. There has been a tendency to undervalue care, perhaps because a large amount of caring in our society is done by women. Much of it is unpaid: caring for children, the sick, disabled or elderly members of family. Where it is paid it is mostly classed as low-skilled work with poor rates of pay. Yet care is important, and we see its centrality in parish ministry reflected in the traditional terminology present in the bishop's charge to a new incumbent: receive this cure of souls, which is yours and mine. This term 'cure', from which we get 'curate' and 'curator', comes from the Latin verb *curo*, which the *Oxford Latin Dictionary* defines thus: 'take care of, mind; worry or care about; order; attend to; heal; cure'. Thus a priest who takes on this charge is committing herself to taking care of, worrying about, attending to and minding these people and this place. She is accepting a responsibility to care for the souls in this place.

Care is a vital aspect of human society. Taking care of people, worrying about them, attending to them, healing them, involves relating to real people in concrete situations. It requires both a being towards people in a caring attitude and a doing of caring things. So if the charge of a parish priest is understood as care, it involves relating caringly to a particular set of people in a particular place. Good experiences of care are shaped by attitudes towards those being cared for, as much as actual functions, and these can be harder to measure in abstract ways. Good care is recognized and appreciated even though at times it is hard to distil into words. We see in current debates around the role of nurses how an overemphasis on measurable targets can come at the expense of humane care, which is far harder to quantify. Care is often linked to virtues which are prominent in the Christian tradition: love, patience, kindness, humility and self-control.

The parish priest holds this responsibility to care within a community whose members are committed to mutual care. The Christian faith exhorts us both to love God and also to love our neighbour. We all have, as those who follow the leadership of Christ, a responsibility to care for those within our Christian family and those beyond the doors of the church. We noted earlier that the sacramental life of the Church needed a priest so that the grace of God could be manifested in the waters of baptism, the elements of communion, the words of absolution and blessing.

Yet we also need to affirm that the grace of God is made manifest in the wider ministry of the Church through all of its members. The theologian Karl Rahner maintains that the grace of God is present in the world through genuine acts of loving compassion and kindness. It is through these caring human encounters that we become channels for God's grace, ministering his love in the world. It is through the compassionate ways Christians care for each other and care for those beyond the Church that the love of God proclaimed is also experienced. We cannot from our human perspective delineate which of our human acts are grace-filled, but we can trust that in our efforts to care for each other we are following in the way of Christ's ministry. The life of a church community needs the sacramental ministry of a priest and the ordinary human ministry of each of its members, including the priest. The sacramental ministry is a means of sustaining and inspiring the ministry of all. The human ministry of compassionate caring bears witness to the God known in the sacraments.

The priest's charge suggests that, for her, the care of the whole parish must be a primary focus. She must utilize her gifts and develop skills in order to help the collective ministry of the church develop and grow. She cannot compel people to play their part to the full, but she does play a pivotal part in sustaining a community in which people find themselves more and more able to live authentically Christian lives. In Ephesians 4, when Paul lists the gifts of apostles, teachers, prophets and evangelists, roles we would associate to some extent with the ordained, he writes that they are for equipping the saints for the work of ministry, for building up the body of Christ, that we all might grow up, mature in faith. This deepening discipleship is linked to mission. The church community is to be a place in which all the saints are able to mature in their faith, so that they may live Christian lives that witness to the graciousness of God.

The church as family

Understanding the church in this way as a caring community in which people grow up and develop their own capacities to care means that it is more like a family than a business. Like a family, we do not select and employ those we are in community with; we make the best of what we have been given. We often talk about the church community in terms of a family and this seems an appropriate image, as the family is at best the place in which we grow up, developing the virtues and values that enable us to reach maturity. Within a family we learn language: our mother tongue. We also learn our manners, ways of being and behaving towards other people and other things. We are cared for and learn how to care. We learn through a complex mixture of copying, following instructions, subliminal reinforcement and deliberate discipline. We learn through trial and error, and we learn best where there is forgiveness and understanding for our failings and delight and encouragement for our success. And, because we are each unique individuals, we also shape and alter the language and manners of the family by our developing personality and all that we bring into the mix.

As a parent, what we hope for in our children is that the language, values and manners they have learnt in the household will fit them to take their place in the wider world, behaving in ways that, though unique to them, accord with the values we have tried to instil. Encounters in and beyond the home will all play their part in this process, but those who have primary responsibility for the care of a child will play a pivotal role. The pivotal role the priest, who is in charge, plays in the family of the church is one of the reasons that the title 'father' has been traditionally used for a priest.

This long-standing metaphor suggests that a priest taking on the charge to care for these people and this place is being like a father, overseeing and caring for his household. Within Roman Catholicism, where celibacy is a requirement of ordination, a priest is understood to forgo an actual family, the better to be able to be the father of a church community. Yet there are difficulties in simply equating the role of priest to a father. There is a theological problem, which arises out of the fact that God is consistently imaged and addressed as our father. The confusion possible in addressing both God and priest as father can too easily suggest that the priest is more like God than the laity. There is also an issue about how we have traditionally understood the role of father in the family. Fathers have been primarily understood as those who leave the domestic setting and work beyond it. They provide financially for their families but are less likely to be engaged in the minutiae of domestic life. Although this understanding of fatherhood is changing, we do need to acknowledge that child rearing and domestic work are still mostly undertaken by women and are perceived of and valued as women's work.

I suggest that it is this domestic and nurturing role which is most akin to the role of a parish priest: the role we traditionally associate with mothers. The church is the community we come to for sustenance, for support and reassurance, so that we might be sent out into the world. Like a home, we return to it in order constantly to go out from it. If we think of the priest playing the role we traditionally associate with a mother in a home, we can enrich our understanding of what it is to be in charge.

Like a mother

Mothering is associated with a way of being in charge that is characterized by love, care and a desire for individuals to flourish. It connects to ideas about home, the place in which we are fed and nurtured, from which we can leave to play our part in the world and to which we can return when the world is a confusing and exhausting place. I acknowledge that not all mothering lives up to this ideal, yet I maintain that this image provides rich resources to help us reflect afresh on the role of a parish priest.

It is important to stress that in using this feminine image of mothering I am not making any claims about the gender of a parish priest. Nor am I suggesting that those who are mothers make better priests. To use a metaphor is to say that something is like something else, and I am suggesting that men and women in their role as parish priests are like mothers in their role in creating and sustaining family life. It is interesting to note that Paul felt comfortable using maternal metaphors to describe his own ministry. In 1 Thessalonians 1.7–8 he talks about his care and concern for that community being like a woman breastfeeding her own children. Beverly Gaventa explores this and other occasions where Paul uses maternal imagery and concludes:

> Maternal imagery appears in contexts referring to the ongoing nature of the relationship between Paul and the congregations he founded; paternal imagery, by contrast, regularly refers to the initial stage of Christian preaching and conversion.[7]

Although such maternal imagery has never been a large part of the language about ministry, it has been used in the past by a number of male writers thinking about their role as abbots or prelates.[8] There has also been a strong tradition that images the Church itself as a mother, nurturing, caring for and feeding her children. In the rest of the book I will explore aspects of this maternal caring and reflect on how it can help us find a richer language to describe what clergy do.

It is often suggested to me that I could remove any issues of gender by using the gender-neutral term 'parenting' rather than 'mothering'. I would certainly acknowledge that the increasing use of this term has been important in showing how the skills of bringing up children can be taught and learnt: that they are not simply an outworking of a female instinct. Men and women can learn the human skills necessary for caring for children and running a home. However, 'parenting' does not yet convey the warmth of relationship and ordinariness of 'mothering' and it lacks the rich traditional resonances. More importantly, its gender-neutrality hides the reality that the care of children and homemaking are undervalued because associated with women. And the undervaluing of this caring plays a vital part in the undervaluing in so many aspects of care beyond the home. I would maintain that if a child only has one parent, whatever the gender of that parent, the role will look like mothering unless the mothering role has been passed on to a paid carer or alternative family member.

The devaluing of caring roles in our society, because they are associated with the domestic and the feminine, has implications for the caring nature of a priest's work and increasingly for the way it is valued. Priests are traditionally involved in areas of work that are associated with the feminine. They spend time with the sick, the sorrowing and the dying. They work with mothers and young children. In our society religion is often associated with the domestic and the feminine. In a society that devalues this work, it is tempting for clergy to look for patterns of ministry that equate more readily to valued ways of working. Thus it can be tempting to find projects that have tangible outcomes and neat timescales, which reduce the time spent in the less easily quantifiable caring activities. However, the reality for most parish clergy is that time is spent in lots of activities that can appear non-productive. How do we quantify the value of visiting the elderly or spending time chatting to mums in the toddler group, to parishioners in the street or to the dying and bereaved?

It is also important at this point to acknowledge that in drawing parallels between mothering and ministry I am not suggesting that clergy are adults to congregational children. There is a proper concern that parental imagery for clergy may imply a desire to infantilize the laity. Clearly, any parish priest will be ministering in a community where people are more mature both in years and in their Christian discipleship. Individuals will be more experienced in aspects of parish ministry, whether that is in terms of managing buildings, money, chairing meetings, visiting the sick or sitting with the dying. Many will have far more experience of the local community, its history and its current complexities. Sensible clergy are fully aware of this and draw on the wisdom, experience and spiritual resources to build up the ministry of the church. Within the parish many of the relationships a priest has will be relationships of mutuality as she works collaboratively with others.

Yet within the church community people will be dependent on the priest for some things most of the time and in other ways for specific periods. These issues will be explored in more detail in later chapters. At this point it is important to note that mothers do not usually aim to keep their children overly dependent. Most mothers want their children to grow up and mature, delighting in the signs of developing independence while deepening a relationship which becomes more mutual. Part of society's devaluing of maternal care is the characterization of a domineering mother who infantilizes her offspring. This may be true of some mothering but it is a distortion to be guarded against, not an inevitability of the relationship.

Conclusion

So what do clergy do? Parish priests are called to be professionals who work within a profession which is hard to define. It does not conform to other professions in terms of rewards, structures and easily defined skills. There are aspects of parish work that are easier to delineate as work. There are services taken – Sunday and midweek services in church, funerals, baptisms and weddings – all of which are offered to other people and recognized as something particular to clergy, akin to a professional skill. There are practical ways in which the church and other associated buildings need to be maintained and managed. Again, such things can be assessed. Yet central to ministry is the building up of the relationships, the quality of incidental encounters, the time spent in praying for people, the care given in walking with people through difficult circumstances and the witness that all of this is connected to the love of God known through Jesus Christ. Such things are hard to quantify, and often the outcomes of such encounters are not obvious in the short term, and may never be recognized this side of heaven.

Like mothering, there is a sense in which the work of clergy is never done. It may contain projects that can be finished, but each project should be feeding into the continuing work of building up a church community in and through which people experience the grace of God, minister that grace in the world and bear witness to the gospel. It is a service industry in which people repeatedly come to be fed and cleansed and sent out, with the priest having responsibility for the quality of such service. It is a creative enterprise where the priest is constantly seeking to weave together the continuing stories of people's lives with the story of God. If done well it takes considerable time and effort. It can be frustrating and deeply rewarding. Yet if it is done well it can also appear to be natural, making it hard for clergy to take credit for all the effort they have put in.

A parish priest is in charge of a parish or set of parishes. This does not mean that she is the boss. To come to the role with that as a model will leave the clergy and congregation frustrated, because the Church is not a business organization. It may make some aspects of the role easier to manage, but ministry is a complex collective collaboration in which clergy have limited power properly to assess, compel or dismiss those who make up the community for which they have a charge. Instead, I suggest, they are more akin to a mother who maintains a home in which her family can be fed, nurtured, loved and cared for and from which they can go out into the wider world. In that wider world they bear the stamp of the home that formed them and continues to sustain them, living out of the beliefs, values and behaviour they have learnt to inhabit. As in any home, many tasks can and should be shared, ideas and ways of behaving are debated and sometimes modified and the whole is a constantly adapting community as its members grow in mutual understanding and care. As and when, the family expands with new members. Having a charge for such a home therefore requires flexibility, adaptability and a desire to collaborate. The rest of this book will attempt to explore some of what such caring responsibility consists of.

2

A relationship and an activity

In becoming a mother I entered a relationship with a child whom we named Ben. My mothering has been developed in relationship with him and with my other son, Joe. To say I am a mother at one level begs the question whose mother I am. I have been a parish priest in Bedford and Sheffield. In each case the role I had was shaped by the actual communities I was licensed to serve. I was a curate of St Andrews, Bedford, vicar of Holy Trinity, Millhouses. My priestly ministry was carried out in these places with these communities. The insights and practices I have learnt in caring for my children can be used when I find myself at times caring for other people's children, but the responsibility is different. Currently I occasionally help out as a priest in some parishes and draw on the skills I developed in parish ministry, but again my relationship and responsibility are not the same.

Mothering and parish ministry are both shaped by the particularity of a given relationship. A bishop charges a priest with the cure of souls of a particular parish or group of parishes. From that point until she leaves, she is in a relationship with these people and places. She is their priest and they are her charge. She is their priest, but she also needs to act as their priest. Being and doing are interwoven. There are plenty of tasks to be done but a list of tasks cannot adequately define the role. Both mothering and ministry are relationships and activities: the relationship shapes the activity and the activity enhances the relationship. In order to explore this idea further I will draw on the work of three very different writers.

The first, Hannah Arendt, was a political philosopher who in *The Human Condition* defines human activity in three realms.[1] Her ideas help to describe the kinds of activity involved in both mothering and ministry. Second, I will outline the concept of maternal practice put forward by Sara Ruddick in *Maternal Thinking*. Her understanding of mothering provides insights that can help in exploring further the ways in which parish ministry is like mothering. Both of these provide ways of looking at mothering which can help us understand the concept of being 'good enough', a term for ordinary mothers coined by the paediatrician Donald Winnicott. This then offers a way into thinking about being good enough clergy. Being good enough involves living by virtues rather than rules, so the last part of the chapter will offer a way of understanding virtue in ministerial practice. The theory in this chapter underpins the ideas in the following chapters which look in more detail at particular issues in the practice of parish ministry.

The centrality of relationship

A priest is the vicar of this parish; that is a fact. He or she has been licensed by the bishop, inducted and installed. The relationship is now a given and priest and people need to learn how to be church together in this place. There are specific things that need to be done by any parish priest and there are particular things that need to be done in this place. What matters is that what is done happens in a way that strengthens the relationship between priest and people and enables them all to minister as the body of Christ in this place. A priest could conduct all necessary services, chair appropriate meetings and visit parishioners but do so in a way that does not enable the people to flourish and grow in their faith. The attitude and character of the priest are fundamental to how her priestly doing is received by those among whom she ministers. This is a relationship.

The Church of England has always held to the theological under-standing that a priest is only a priest for people. A priest is ordained to a title, grounding her priestly ministry in the reality of a particular relationship: these people, this place. The sacramental ministry of a priest always involves at least one other person. There is no tradition of private mass. Even when a priest has a general licence, a permission to officiate, the occasions on which she performs priestly ministry are with and for actual people. It is a concrete, contextual reality, not an abstract one. This being and doing relationship is also central to mothering.

A mother is a mother of certain children and her mothering is shaped by the reality of those children and the things she does for them and the way they respond to her doing. I am Ben's and Joe's mother. Their sense of what a mother is and how a mother should be has been shaped by the particular experience of how I relate to them and what I do for them. The kind of mother I am has in part been shaped by these particular children. I have consistently done enough maternal things, with a loving caring attitude, for them to trust me and respect me as their mother.

For complex reasons, my own mother left the family home when I, my sisters and brother were still quite young. Although she in some sense continues to be my mother, she has in fact for a large part of my life done little in the way of mothering. Here, the title 'mother' has become divorced from the activity and embodiment of mothering. Similarly, and only a few centuries ago, parishioners would often complain, about absent clergy, that their vicar was not their parish priest – these duties often being delegated to a poor curate, or sometimes to no one at all. As with 'mother', the title 'vicar' may be retained, but without an engaged and sustained relationship for those in our care the term becomes divorced from the activities that define the essence and character of the term. To be a good enough vicar will mean ministering well, inhabiting the term and embodying the intentional virtues of the title. Similarly, to be a good enough mother will mean mothering well. The activity is necessary for the relationship to be meaningful.

Hannah Arendt – labour, work and action

So how can we better understand this being and doing that interconnect in the role of parish priest? I have found it helpful to use the work of the political philosopher Hannah Arendt in trying to understand the activity that makes up the doing of both mothering and parish ministry. In her book *The Human Condition* she divides human activity into three different realms. First there is all that is necessary for human life to be sustained, and this she calls *labour*. Labouring encompasses the everyday tasks that must be done but can be shared out. In the domestic setting these tasks will include cooking, feeding, washing and tidying, all necessary for the continuing life of the home.

Her second category describes the making of things, which she calls *work* or *fabrication*. Here the end justifies the means and the end is a tangible product. This is the world of craftsmen who produce things that will last. This kind of work suits target setting and measurable outcomes because it is about making tangible things. Her third category is *action*, by which she means all that goes into building up human communities: politics in the widest sense of that word. In the realm of action, relationships matter; it is about how we speak to others and build up our understanding of them and their understanding of us.

Arendt was writing as a political theorist. Yet I find her categories helpful in looking at the roles of mothering and parish ministry. Both, I suggest, involve a complex mix of labouring and action. There are aspects of what Arendt calls work, but this realm is not as central to these roles as labour and action. In both mothering and ministry we find many tasks that need to be done to sustain life and maintain the home or church. Some of these are mundane and routine; they are domestic tasks such as feeding, washing and tidying up. Yet such tasks are interwoven with the building up of the community, the development of relationships that enable people to work together, to grow in understanding others and in self-understanding. This interweaving of labouring and action offers a different way of expressing the entwined being and doing of mothering and ministry. As we saw in the last chapter, neither is principally involved with making products so neither occupation can be fully appraised by measures designed to assess tangible outcomes.

Sara Ruddick – maternal thinking

We rarely describe mothering as a profession. We do acknowledge that it can be an occupation but, perhaps most importantly, it is understood as a way of life that is practised. That is, it is learnt by the doing and the reflecting on the doing. And the doing is always done in order to enhance and develop the relationship. So if we can talk about ministry being like mothering, then I suggest that understanding what it means to describe mothering as a practice can help us explore the practice of a priest in parish ministry. To do this I will draw on the work of Sara Ruddick, whose book *Maternal Thinking* sets out to describe the reasoning implicit in mothering. At the basis of her work is an understanding of a practice as an activity that is shaped by particular goals and demands. She gives the simple example of horse racing.

> Horse racing, for example, is defined by the goal of winning a race by means of riding a horse over a finish line ... A horse racing riderless past the wire, and a jockey slowing her mount in the interest of its beauty are not engaged in horse racing ... To be recognized as a jockey ... means to evince or to pretend a commitment to crossing the finish line.[2]

This is a fairly simple practice with a clear goal: winning a race on a horse. An activity like mothering is, of course, more complex; its goal is to enable another human being to develop towards maturity, and Ruddick suggests that this goal is shaped by a threefold set of demands. That is, there are three overlapping concerns that drive what a mother does, and these feel like demands because they arise out of the responsibility she has for a vulnerable person's life. They are all good but they are often in tension, which makes mothering a complex practice. So what are these three demands?

The most basic demand that a child presents a mother with is its need to be kept alive and safe. Ruddick calls this first demand 'preservation'. Meeting this demand involves the mother in many activities that ensure the child is fed and kept warm and safe from harm. It can be characterized by the image of a mother holding a child in her arms: that sense of protection and loving commitment. The goal is that the child will be kept safe. Yet this aim to keep the child safe and secure sits alongside a second demand to foster his growth. Children need to grow up and explore, to take risks and to leave the security of their mother's arms. This letting go and encouraging development happens in different ways at different stages of the child's life. The mother lets the child stumble across the floor with his first steps, allowing for possible bumps and tears, just as she will in time pack him off to new places and adventures where she will not be able to watch over his every move and catch him when he falls. Children need support and encouragement to explore the world and develop their own capacities. Holding a child safe is central to mothering but so is letting go, because the goal is that the child will survive and become mature.

The third demand comes not so much from the child but from the reality that we live in social contexts and a child needs to find his place in society. Ruddick calls it 'acceptability'.

> Many mothers find that the central challenge of mothering lies in training a child to be the kind of person whom others accept and whom the mothers themselves can actively appreciate.[3]

The aim is that the child will be safe and will grow towards maturity, and will do so in such a way that he can live well with those around him, understanding the social nature of human existence. Thus mothers teach manners, doing their best to inculcate the kind of values and behaviour that will allow their child to get on with people and understand how to be in the world which he must inhabit.

These three demands are intertwined in the daily practice of mothering but they are quite often in conflict. Should I discourage my son from climbing the tree in case he falls or should I risk the possibility of an injury to enable him to explore and learn more about his body and his world? What if he is with other children who cannot explore in this way, or if he is inappropriately dressed, or the tree is on the neighbour's property? Judgements need to be made that are shaped by the contingent reality of the situation; on this day in this place with this child, which seems the most appropriate demand to meet? There are no generically right answers, but wisdom can be built up through practice, enabling a mother to make good judgements. Thus mothers at best develop a practical wisdom: that is, a wisdom which arises out of what they do and their ability to reflect on and learn from what they do. This wisdom is a virtue, a developed capacity to make wise decisions in concrete situations; in Aristotle's traditional terminology it is called *phronesis*, sometimes translated as 'prudence'.

This way of looking at mothering focuses less on describing the tasks involved and more on the thinking which precedes and shapes the activity. It acknowledges that different mothers will respond to these demands in different ways. Yet there is a coherent recognition between mothers that what they are trying to do is keep their children safe while encouraging them to grow up, and doing so within a social setting which sets its own criteria of acceptable behaviour. Mothering is not simply the response to a maternal instinct.

There are aspects of the care and nurture of children that do connect to instinctual behaviour. A baby's cry is designed to evoke a response; a lactating mother may find her milk begins to flow. She knows instinctively that the baby needs feeding but, as many mothers will confirm, she needs to learn how to hold and position the baby aright in order to feed the hungry infant satisfactorily. She knows that the infant needs to be kept clean and warm but she learns how to do this by watching others, taking advice, and with a certain amount of trial and error.

As babies become infants, children and on to adolescents, the process of caring for them continues to involve learning through a mixture of guesswork, advice, shared wisdom, trial and error, and negotiation. Mothering is a learnt practice. Like all learning it comes more easily to some than others. Aspects beyond the mother–child relationship also impact on this learning. Issues of security, access to support and equipment, previous experience and the capacity for reflective learning will all make a difference for how maternal practice develops. There are no blueprints and perfection is unobtainable; the aim is to be good enough.

Donald Winnicott – an ordinary good enough mother

The concept of being a 'good enough' mother was developed by the paediatrician Donald Winnicott in the 1950s.[4] He argued that a mother must be responsive to the needs of her child, but she cannot, and more importantly should not, perfectly anticipate and meet every need a baby has. It is in the realizations that not every need is met by the mother that a child begins to learn to do things himself and to develop capacities that lead to maturity. A good enough mother responds appropriately on enough occasions for the child to feel secure. On the occasions when she does not, he begins to learn to manage his own feelings and develop his own capacities to calm himself down or meet his own needs.

Ruddick's concept of maternal demands, explained in the previous section, makes the impossibility of meeting all a child's needs clear. These threefold demands are often in tension; to meet one aspect may mean frustrating another. Thus it follows that to meet every need for security would mean always attempting to prioritize preservation over fostering growth. A mother could always dress her child and often it may seem speedier to do so, but there comes an important point where she encourages him to do it himself, and sometimes even insists on that in the face of complaint and resistance. In this case the desire to foster his growth and develop skills considered appropriate for his age overrides the desire to keep him happy.

To be good enough is to be consistent enough in meeting a child's needs so that he can trust his mother, but allowing him to develop capacities of his own so that he can mature. Winnicott writes:

> Mothers with babies are dealing with a developing changing situation; the baby starts off not knowing about the world, and by the time they have finished their job the baby is grown into someone who knows about the world and can find a way to live in it, and even to take part in the way it behaves. What a tremendous development![5]

It requires judgement on a mother's part to know when to hold him close and when and how to let him go and grow. It requires wisdom and discernment to help him find his place in the world. Through the building up of experience, the thinking involved in such judgements becomes habitual and a mother may not even consider it a form of reasoning; it may begin to feel instinctual.

Yet it is a form of reasoning. This is a way of reasoning that is rooted in concrete thinking. It is also a way of reasoning that holds together thinking and feeling. There is a tendency to value abstract thinking above concrete thinking and to maintain that feelings get in the way of reason. Yet there are many situations where abstract thinking is simply inappropriate and detachment unhelpful. Real children, real people, are unique. They may be like another person in many aspects, they may be behaving in ways we have seen and experienced before, but each encounter requires us to respond to the reality of this child at this moment in this place. Strategies that may have worked with one child may not with another. If the child is tired, hungry or overexcited he will need different responses from when he is settled and well fed. Responses that are appropriate at home may be inappropriate in the middle of a shopping centre or while driving down a motorway.

Thus a mother has to think about the best way to deal with him in this mood, in this place, on this occasion. The ideal scenario described in the childcare books or outlined by her friends may be very different from the one she is facing. Mothers have to think on the hoof. This thinking, this practical reasoning, uses feelings as a way of assessing action. The tendency to separate feelings from reason presumes that dispassionate thinking is of a higher quality than emotional reasoning. Yet if we look at mothering we see how vital feelings are to making the kinds of practical on-the-hoof judgements discussed above.

A child cries because he feels unhappy; the mother responds to the unhappiness of the child, feeling concerned and worried for him; she is emotionally moved. She reasons, thinking about what it might be that is distressing him: is he scared, hungry, hurt or just very tired? She decides how to act, prioritizing her actions, perhaps comforting first then ascertaining what might move him into a better place. She then reads his feelings: does he look less distressed, has he calmed down and how does she feel? Is he now safe and content? A mother feels the needs of the child and this motivates her to think about how best to respond; she then assesses her response by seeing how the child feels and how she feels about the child. This is the appropriate blending of reasoning and feeling for an occupation that is focused on the care of a real human being.

Being good enough parish priests

I have spent some time describing the demands and thinking involved in mothering because there are some important parallels with parish ministry. As I noted in the previous chapter, the New Testament suggests in a number of places that the church is the community within which Christians are to grow up and mature. It is a community in which, and for which, the parish priest needs to care. The way Ruddick explains the demands of mothering can, I suggest, help us think about the complex demands of parish ministry. Parish priests, like mothers, often feel that the job is never done and they may struggle to evaluate properly what they are doing. As a parish priest there were days when all I could see were the things I had failed to do, the visits not made, the follow-up that did not happen or the creative initiative that never got out of my head. I knew I was not perfect. Could the concept of being good enough provide a more honest understanding and evaluation of the role of parish clergy? Exploring how Ruddick's ideas map on to parish life can help articulate what a good enough priest is called to do.

The threefold demands of parish ministry

The demands that Ruddick describes in mothering seem to offer a way of articulating the tensions in ministry and this sense of never managing to get everything right. A priest is called on to preserve the life and faith of individuals and communities. There is a responsibility to keep things going, to provide the necessary sustenance so that people may be fed and cared for. The life of a given church needs to be maintained. There is, in Arendt's terminology, a labouring aspect to this. Yet the routine labouring is also about developing and sustaining the relationships necessary for community: it is interwoven with action. This sustaining and nurturing of the life of a congregation and a parish takes up much of a priest's time. It involves both the practical tasks necessary for the continuing life of services and the pastoral care of those for whom she is responsible. A priest is called on to hold these people metaphorically, to hold them in her heart.

Yet this church and these people need to grow, mature and develop in their faith. This means that the priest needs to challenge people, encourage them to think, to explore, take risks and accept new responsibilities. She needs to ensure that people are developing and using their gifts and strengths, doing some things for themselves and doing things for others. The community must be helped to adjust to new members, new circumstances and the complex reality of the wider world. There is a demand to foster growth in the church and in the lives of those for whom she is responsible. There is a demand for deepening discipleship and engagement in outreach and mission. People need to be sent out.

Ruddick describes how, for mothers, the demands of preservation and fostering growth are often in tension. This is also true for parish clergy. The security people find in the familiar aspects of church life is comforting and sustaining. The community needs the necessities of life, the feeding in word and sacrament, the favourite hymns and music, the friendly faces and reassuring sense of belonging. When faced with things that are overwhelming in their personal life or in the wider world they want to be metaphorically held: held by the rituals of the church, the reassurances of the clergy, the underpinning of who they are, by love, care and prayer.

Yet alongside this sense of being securely held, the church is a place where they should be encouraged to grow up in faith. They need to have a diet that allows for variety within the familiar, that stretches the palate, helping people to think deeply about their discipleship. They need to be encouraged to take responsibility for their faith and to play their part in bearing witness to it. The New Testament tells us that the church is a community in which its members should grow up, aiming for maturity in Christ. Churches should be growing communities with new people coming in and changing things by their presence.

The holding and preserving of people's faith alongside the challenging encouragement towards growth and maturity all happens within the wider context of the particular denomination and tradition. There are boundaries which are set by the local and wider church on what is and is not acceptable. These may in some cases be challenged and refined, but they need to be understood by Christians. Christianity is a social religion; being part of the fellowship, working alongside other Christians in the ministry of the church, is part of discipleship. Priests need to teach people what is acceptable, always aware that they may need to rethink and modify these boundaries as they learn more about people and their lives.

For Christians, though, acceptability is not just about getting along with other Christians. It is about providing a consistent and coherent witness to the wider world. It is also, perhaps most importantly, about being acceptable to God. Helping individuals and communities to live up to God's standards and to fit themselves for the kingdom of heaven can be a complex aspect of the prophetic ministry of a priest. The New Testament is clear that there is a great responsibility on those who teach and shape the Christian faith of others.

The role of clergy is more complex than mothering because they are helping and shaping a whole community, while caring for the many different individuals who make up that community. Within an ordinary parish church there will be individuals who need to be held safe, whose experience of life means that they are like a bruised reed or a flickering wick. They need to be treated gently. Others will need to be challenged and drawn out, encouraged to grow in their faith. Some will need to be gently reminded of boundaries or of how to dwell well together with those who are different. This means that a priest needs to be constantly drawing on the kind of practical reasoning that allows her to prioritize and respond appropriately. This involves concrete thinking and a proper use of feelings in developing appropriate action. She will not always get it right but she needs to get it right often enough to be trusted.

A parish priest is doing her best to hold together a community with different needs, trying to enable a diverse mix of people to understand how to be the Church together in this place. It is not possible to find perfect answers; living in community involves a certain level of compromise and cooperation. In some circumstances keeping people safe may be prioritized over encouraging their growth, but it must not be prioritized simply for an easier life or out of a fear of allowing people to think for themselves. Thinking about growth is important, but in reaching out to others in mission there needs to be a realistic presentation of what is expected of Christian discipleship; grace is free but discipleship may well be costly.

The kind of scenario that is familiar to most parishes might involve the old and the very young. It is wonderful that Mary comes to church each week with her young son Joshua. She is not really from a churchgoing family but ever since the baptism service she has done her best to be here. For Jack and Vera the presence of Joshua is a strain. Mary does not control him the way they controlled their children. He makes a noise at inappropriate moments and distracts them from the service. This weekly service is central to their life and faith; the church is a space in which they feel close to God, and hearing the word and receiving communion sustains them. Another close friend died recently and they feel old and very mortal. Vera thinks Mary should simply stay home until Joshua is older. Jack thinks she should give him a smack. The priest thinks, 'Thank goodness for Mary, a sign of new life. How can I continue to make her welcome? What can I do about the black looks she gets?' And at times the priest thinks, 'Why can't she pack quieter toys for him or persuade him to sit a little stiller?'

Mary, Jack, Vera and Joshua all need to be held secure in their faith, yet all also need to grow in understanding of God and of each other. The priest needs to find the wisdom that can help them, knowing when to affirm and when to challenge, how to help the church community adjust to changes in parenting and help a newcomer understand the rhythms of a service and the needs of other people. It may mean practical adjustments to the space, issues around what is provided for young children. It may mean time spent helping Mary think about how to be with Joshua in the church. It might need time with Jack and Vera, thinking about how they can be part of the ministry of the church in the way they make newcomers welcome and help to settle them in. There are no easy answers, but there is deep skill in a priest who finds ways to balance the needs so that all feel they can worship together.

In parish ministry there is rarely a clear right answer; the way forward needs to be thought through. Sometimes this takes time, sometimes it needs to happen quickly, but this thinking always requires concrete reasoning and a proper synthesis of reason and feeling. There are abstract principles and models that can help in thinking through concrete experiences but each situation is unique and therefore needs a unique response. It may be like other responses but it needs to be thought through for this place and people at this time. Those we know well can be challenged more readily than those we are just encountering. Understanding people's stories helps us to think more deeply about how they will react to things and when they will need careful holding or an encouraging push. Thus ministry is more of an art than a science.

It is in the nature of the role to get it wrong sometimes. People and situations will on occasions be misread, signs missed and mistakes made. Practical wisdom is developed through a certain amount of trial and error. This requires the ability to be honest about failings and use them as ways of building up wisdom. It is a reflective way of reasoning that takes seriously how people are feeling and uses feelings as a way of assessing appropriate responses. It acknowledges that perfection is not possible because there is an inherent tension in the demands of ministry. Seeking to be good enough is not settling for mediocrity. Being good enough acknowledges the internal conflicts present in a role that is about people and caring for people, in all the complexity of their competing needs. Being good enough is what enables others to grow and mature, providing enough security without smothering them.

Practising virtues

As I said above, ministry is an art rather than a science: it cannot be carried out successfully by following rules or generic patterns. In place of rules it needs the development of virtues. Virtues in common Christian parlance tend to have a rather sterile feel to them, which has not been helped by the partnering of virtues with specific vices. The implication of this is that virtue is simply the opposite of vice, a rather unobtainable perfection. However, there is a richer way of understanding virtue, which we find if we go back to Aristotle.

He describes a virtue not as an opposite of a vice but as a balance between an excess or deficiency of the virtue. A given virtue is a mathematical mean between two failures of virtue which fall either side. Thus courage is the virtue that lies between rashness and cowardice: rashness is an excess and cowardice a lack, and both are failures of virtue. What courage is cannot really be defined in the abstract because the actual situation will determine what is courageous; it is not possible to say in advance of a situation what will be courage and what rashness or cowardice. A judgement needs to be made which weighs up the given situation in all its complexity. An individual who is courageous will think through this judgement extremely quickly – it may even seem instinctual, but she will have used the wisdom she has built up to make the choice of how to act.

Developing the ability to be good enough in either ministry or mothering means developing virtues rather than following rules. Earlier in this chapter I noted the virtue Aristotle called *phronesis*, which is translated as 'prudence' or 'practical wisdom'. Unfortunately 'prudence' has taken on a rather dour and ungracious image, so I will stick to the translation 'practical wisdom'. This is the virtue that is built up by being involved in a particular practice, enabling an individual to make good judgements about how to act within that practice, almost instantaneously.

In mothering, as a mother begins to get used to her child she builds up practical wisdom. She has learnt some of it from other mothers, other children and books about mothering, but much has been worked out by a trial and error process of what does and does not work to calm this child. She has learnt to read the child, to understand his signals, knowing what is urgent and when he can be left to calm down a bit himself. She knows that holding him in a particular way usually settles him, but she also knows that each day is different and what worked yesterday may not work today. She is trying to balance the different demands of mothering, responding to his needs but not overwhelming him. And the child is always changing, which means his needs are subtly different, requiring a continual learning of practical wisdom as the mother adapts to the growing child.

The reading of the child happens in order that the response is, as often as can be, appropriate. As we have seen, that may be in doing something for the child or it may mean encouraging the child to do something for himself. Being a good enough mother means finding the balance between over-intrusive care and neglect: not attempting to meet every need before the child has expressed it, smothering him, but not neglecting his need. Ruddick suggests that finding this balance requires the development of the virtue humility. She defines humility as the balance between trying to control everything to keep the child safe, which becomes an over-intrusive form of care, and on the other hand an abnegation of responsibility, which is carelessness or at worst neglect.

With 'humility', a mother respects the limits of her will and the independent, uncontrollable, and increasingly separate existence she seeks to preserve. A mother without humility would become frantic in her efforts to protect. But she cannot, out of degenerative humility or passivity, relinquish efforts to control.[6]

By 'control', Ruddick means the responsibility a mother has to keep a child safe, which means that she has to put limits on his freedom. She cannot, in giving in to his will, risk putting him in danger, but nor can she enable him to grow by controlling every aspect of what he does. Humility means having an appropriate assessment of the limits of her power, preventing her from trying to control everything and potentially dominating the child. Yet it is about having a right judgement of what her responsibility is. It would also be a failure in humility to degenerate into a passivity which means she takes no proper responsibility, leading to neglect or to the child inappropriately dominating her.

Rather than talking about vices, when Ruddick outlines a virtue she talks about the degenerative forms of the virtue which pull in either direction. By 'degenerative' she means the ways of acting that do not bring life and flourishing. Being virtuous, finding the appropriate response, is not easy and she suggests that the degenerative forms are often tempting, appearing to offer an easier life or a less contentious way forward. For example, it can be tempting to dominate the child by continuing to do practical things for him rather than find the patience to teach him to do them for himself. Any mother who has seen the painstaking process of a child trying to put on his own shoes knows how tempting it is just to keep doing it for him. The danger is that if this happens all the time he will not develop his own capabilities.

Domination of the child may also come from a mother's fantasy that she can have perfect control over his world; desiring to keep him safe, she might try to minimize all germs, finding it hard to let him play in the mud or pat the neighbour's dogs. Again this is an understandable temptation but may lead to continuing problems as he matures. On the other hand, a mother could move into forms of passivity or neglect because she feels the world is beyond her control and the child simply has to fend for himself. It can be tempting to submit to a particular expert regime rather than trust her own judgement or simply to give in to whatever the child appears to want, leading him to believe that screaming gets results. When she feels powerless and uncertain of her own ability to make good judgements, she may end up abnegating responsibility and in doing so fail to keep her child either safe or acceptable.

Ruddick describes other virtues as important for mothering and in doing so names the temptations to their degenerative forms. She names the virtue of cheerfulness as something which sustains mothers in the continuing work of caring for a child and prevents them from falling into despair about all that they cannot get right or make safe. This virtue also has to guard against the temptation of cheery denial: an unrealistic gloss which cannot deal with the difficult and dark aspects of the role and the world in which she is bringing up her child. Therefore it needs to be clear-sighted resilient cheerfulness, the ability to know the realities of life and to continue doing one's best hopefully.

She describes trust as a necessary virtue which needs to guard against the temptation to require blind obedience from a child or, the opposite temptation, of failing to establish any boundaries within which the child can feel secure. She also talks about realism, delight, attentive love and forgiveness as virtues, and these will in different ways be explored as the book unfolds. Central to her understanding is that 'to name a virtue is not to possess it'. It is, she suggests, about identifying the struggle and acknowledging the temptations, making it more likely that decisions and actions will be appropriate often enough, and, where they are not, helping a mother to acknowledge her faults and try again.

This concept of naming virtues and the temptations that pull in opposite directions is an insightful way of describing the constant process of how to respond well to those we care for. Priests should be comfortable with the idea of temptation and the sense that we fall short of the ideal, through ignorance, weakness and our own deliberate fault. With the competing demands of ministry we need to cultivate virtues in order to prioritize wisely and get it right often enough for enough of the people. There are plenty of temptations to find what appear to be easier routes to getting to a desired end but no shortcuts to the patient work of building up and sustaining the community of the church.

Just as in mothering, the temptation in ministry to over-intrusive care, to dominance, is very real, as is the pull in the other direction towards passivity or neglect. For good reasons a parish priest may feel that her role is to meet everyone's needs all the time and may unwittingly be over-intrusive in her caring. Her need to be needed may create unnecessary dependencies as she prioritizes her holding ministry, finding it hard to let people grow up. It can be tempting to keep doing things for those who need to be learning to do things for themselves, justifying one's importance at the expense of the gifts of others. Clergy can be tempted to discourage theological discussions, preferring to maintain their expertise over the congregation in a form of dominance which discourages mature growth. They may discourage the ministry of others because they cannot control how it is done and it might not be up to their exacting standards. Alternatively they may be tempted into a false humility, equating servanthood with passivity and self-negation. This can lead to an abnegation of responsibility, failing to take decisions or to tackle bad behaviour. A parish can then end up with unhelpful power vacuums, which mean either that things are not done or that others come in to dominate.

As we saw in the first chapter, there is in parish ministry a temptation to be the boss or the servant, but neither is an adequate model to both care for people and enable them to grow and mature. At times, though, both can feel tempting as ways which appear to get the job done or avoid conflict. The danger is that either can in the end become manipulative: degenerate forms of caring which do not help individuals and communities to flourish. Like mothers, clergy need to find the resilient cheerfulness to keep going despite everything, guarding against the temptations of despair or cheery denial.

Virtues are named and cultivated through reflective practice: that is, through being able to reflect on the ups and downs, successes and failures of day-to-day life in the role. They can become habitual so that an individual often enough acts in a virtuous way and becomes less conscious of the thought process involved. They are not personality traits, though some of us will find some virtues easier to cultivate than others. Upbringing and life experience affect our behaviour and can be helps or hindrances in developing the wisdom necessary for the practice.

To be virtuous means understanding the importance of concrete thinking and utilizing feelings as part of reasoning about how to act well in this situation. The role of a parish priest is demanding. Like mothering, it contains internal tensions. This is because it is about a relationship of responsibility to care for real people in real situations. The demand to preserve and sustain the life of the church, while encouraging the growth and maturity of the individuals and community, will often require sensitive prioritizing and careful negotiation. The demands of acceptability require sensitive teaching alongside a humility open to learning new things, sometimes from unexpected sources. In sustaining the relationship into which they have been called, parish clergy need to be good enough. They need to engage in the labouring necessary to create the places and spaces in which these people can feel secure and grow towards maturity. They need to build up the community through collaborative ways of being church, recognizing the uniqueness of these people and this place. It is a relationship and an activity in which the actions develop the relationship and the relationship draws forth the actions.

3

Playing the gift game

———•·•·•———

In idle moments or moments of deep frustration, clergy can fantasize about the kind of congregation and parish they would like to have. It would have a range of people with all the right gifts and experience to make the life of the priest an easier one. There would be gifted musicians who never got difficult, people with real aptitude for working with children and young people, those who simply loved doing church cleaning, church finances and maintenance work! Where decisions were arrived at easily, egos would not need stroking and new people would be easily drawn in. Yet at heart most priests know that this fantasy parish would turn out to have its problems too, because for it to exist the people would be real people and they would surprise, frustrate and change in ways that were unplanned and beyond the priest's control.

In building up relationships, whether in the family or the church, the uniqueness of people means that the outcomes are never fully predictable. One of the strange aspects of mothering is the process of getting to know a child who has been part of you and yet is so utterly other. From the earliest stages the child develops a recognizably individual personality which the mother learns to know and with which she learns to negotiate. If the process of caring for this child is going to work for them both, she needs to tune herself in to the child's temperament just as the child learns to tune himself to his mother. This is a continuing process of negotiating a relationship, of getting to know the other. Some child development writers call this process 'attunement'. Tuning in to this child means learning to know who he is. It means accepting the ways in which he is different from other children she has had, different from the child in the books she has read for advice, and different perhaps from the child she had imagined through all the months of pregnancy.

In this chapter I will look at this process of attunement, which requires the virtue of proper attention, seeing people as they are, not as we fantasize or fear they may be. Not only is it important to try to attend to the uniqueness of each person, we also need to value them. I will suggest that clergy need to learn to play the 'gift game', developing ways of cherishing those for whom they are called to care. Learning to know people and places involves listening to their stories and telling stories together. Listening, chatting and spending time together are important for the development of relationships. Much of this might seem unproductive, but it is central to building up both individuals and communities. Attending to God is necessary, with time spent in listening, chatting and telling stories in prayer and study. The people of her parish are gifts from God and the priest is herself God's gift to this place. Attention is needed so that the gifts are well used for the benefit of all and the flourishing of God's kingdom.

Attention

To pay attention to something or someone is to focus properly; it is about truly seeing what is there and doing one's best to comprehend it. It is active, demanding concentration and energy. Iris Murdoch points out that really attending involves letting go of the fantasies and fears we project on to other people. She maintains that it is not easy to focus and see people as they are and not as we think they are, hope they are or fear they may be.[1] Ruddick draws on Murdoch's ideas to describe the attention aimed at in mothering. This is a loving attention, constantly seeking to respond appropriately to the real child. She calls it a discipline and a virtue: 'Attentive love, or loving attention, represents a kind of knowing that takes truthfulness as its aim but makes truth serve lovingly the person known.'[2]

Attending to a child involves the constant question, 'How is it with you?' This is not necessarily spoken but is an attitude and disposition which is tuned in to the well-being of the child. A mother knows in asking this question that life is constantly changing, presenting new challenges, dangers, joys and blessings for the child to negotiate.

Attention is important in all caring relationships, for adults as well as children, as they negotiate the changing circumstances of life. Attention means a shift of focus on to the reality of the other away from the self. This is necessary in order to feel the other's need, but it cannot be simply equated with self-denial. What is needed is the capacity to focus on the other while retaining the perspective that comes from a secure sense of self. In the previous chapter I noted that in naming a virtue it is helpful to look at the associated temptations.

It is tempting to forgo the effort of proper attention and assume that we already know who this person is and what he or she wants. Such a failure to attend can mean that the person becomes a kind of fantasy person, a 'type' rather than an individual, becoming objectified and turned into a case. Many of us will have experienced this in some areas of life, perhaps in the health service where we become a patient with a particular kind of illness or in other settings where we become identified with our problem rather than encountered as a person. It is at its least frustrating and at its worst dehumanizing. Those engaged in parish ministry need to ensure that pressures of time, or a failure to attend to the uniqueness of each situation, do not lead to treating people or situations as types.

Proper attention also guards against the temptations arising out of lack of self-worth. A deep-seated need to be validated by others may mean that the focus shifts from the one being cared for back on to the carer. In these situations we are made to feel beholden to the one caring, concerned about his or her needs as much, if not more, than our own. It may look like a selfless concern for others but can easily become attention-seeking rather than attentive. Both clergy and mothers need to guard against a perverted self-denial which becomes manipulative.

Proper attention is a disciplined way of seeing the real person and his or her actual needs, making it easier to meet those needs appropriately. Letting go of the fantasies can be hard. A parent may need to let go of her fantasy that her son will be a great sportsman and accept that he would rather have his head in a book, or recognize that he will not achieve in the same way as his brother or cousin or the child down the road. Parish priests may need to accept that this person is not going to take on this area of ministry and does not live up to the hopes they had for him when he joined the church, or that this parish is not going to grow as easily as the last or as vigorously as the one next door, just as congregations need to accept that this priest is not the archangel Gabriel but has feet of clay.

Yet as well as accepting disappointment, as fantasy gives way to reality proper attention can allow a genuine appreciation of the gifts and strengths that are there. These may surprise and delight, offering new ways of understanding success and different visions of the future.

Parents need to learn that children are a gift, not a commodity; despite all parents do to educate and stimulate them, they do not always unfold in expected ways. As clergy develop the capacity to attend well to the people in their care, they need to understand that they too are gifts.

The gift game

At the beginning of this chapter I suggested that clergy sometimes imagine how much easier their life would be if they could select their ideal congregation, but the reality is that we are called to love and care for those we are given. It is with the complex mix of people drawn together as the local church that we are meant to live out our calling to be the body of Christ in this place. In any such community there will be individuals who are easy to recognize as gifts from God and those who are harder to appreciate. Yet we need to care for and value them all. Parish priests need to develop the capacity to play what I call the 'gift game'. Those, like me, who know the children's book *Pollyanna* will be aware of the 'glad game' which Pollyanna's missionary father taught her to play in order to cope with the losses and privations of her young life. She was to reflect on each situation, even the most difficult, and try and find some aspect that she could be glad about and thank God for. Film and TV adaptations of the book have made this seem rather saccharine, but essentially it is an attitude of mind that looks for the goodness of God even in the dark and difficult experiences of life. It is a discipline that is hopeful and redemptive.

Within the church community, I suggest, we need to play a version of this game in which we develop an attitude that sees all those in the congregation as God's gifts to this place and necessary for his work in this place. If we take seriously Paul's metaphor in Romans and Corinthians, which describes the church as a body, then we affirm theologically that each person has his or her part to play in the church's mission and ministry. Each is at some level necessary. It is easy to see some people as gifts, especially if they are those we would naturally befriend, who think like us or generally make our life easier. The discipline comes in letting go of the fantasy congregation and endeavouring to see how those we find it harder to like or value are actually God's gifts, necessary for the life of the Church in this place. This seeing others as gifts to this place and its ministry is not just an attitude for clergy but one that needs to be modelled and taught so that all develop the capacity to value their Christian brothers and sisters. There is something wonderfully counter-cultural about a church community which draws together disparate people, mixing generations and professions and cutting across all sorts of other boundaries of social stratification.

To recognize others as gifts we need to attend to them, to try and see who they are and what they add to the life of the community. In my experience I have found that some of those I initially found harder to like were important correctives to my blind spots and I came to value them for that. Their perspective could help to refine my views. Understanding what mattered to them could help me reflect on what we were doing and being as a church in new ways. Different circumstances in the church's continuing lives can highlight gifts in unexpected people and enable new ways of looking at them and the ministry of the whole.

Ruddick and Murdoch link attention to the virtue of love. To speak of loving attention towards a child makes sense, but it can seem much harder to explore the concept of loving attention when we are talking about a whole community of people for whom a priest carries responsibility. It is unlikely that we will learn to love everyone! However, where love does not flow easily we need to develop a capacity to treat others as if we do love them. This as an ethical stance, but for Christians it is also a theological stance. We value others as those who are deeply beloved of God. Like ourselves, these individuals are loved by God despite their faults and God can and will use them as a means of his grace and a part of his continuing work in the world. Sometimes we need to pray for the ability to see others as God's gifts and the capacity to respond to them as those who are precious to God. Recognizing that each person is a precious individual given to this community by God should help guard against treating them as types. Knowing that she is loved and valued by God should help the priest find the security in her own self, so that she can care generously without being tempted to validate herself through the needs of others.

The art of cherishing

Understanding people as gifts reminds us that one of the key roles of a parish priest is to cherish the people in her care. Jesus' parable of the lost sheep reminds us that we do not work with an attitude of natural wastage; he cherishes each and every one. For people to feel cherished they need, as we have already noted, to be recognized and treated as unique, not simply as a type. Each one is a person, not a case. Clearly the number of people that a given priest is responsible for has implications for the way such cherishing is manifested. In small congregations it is easy to know people's names, their families and concerns. In larger congregations and communities, where many feel anonymous beyond the church, strategies may be needed to ensure that people feel cherished.

As a curate I was taught by the vicar to learn the names of the congregation so that I could administer at the communion rail using their name. This was a thriving church with three services of Holy Communion on a Sunday. It was a discipline to learn the names. Yet as he pointed out, it meant that even in the busyness and rush of these large congregations each one had been recognized as an individual, noted and named. Each one was a unique person. As a student in Cambridge I remember the skill of the then Vicar of Holy Trinity Church speaking to people after the service, making connections with the many visitors, remembering who had been before, making people feel valued. In contrast I know I am not the only one to have attended a church with my husband and a young baby where nobody spoke to us after the service to enquire who we were or whether we were new to the area. Most congregations take seriously the welcoming of newcomers, but it is also vitally important to continue to find constructive ways to value the regulars, especially those who are perhaps less able to give time and energy to the church through age, infirmity or life commitments beyond the parish.

Here good administration plays a key role. Parish priests need to find ways that work for them to remember names, family details and important anniversaries in the lives of the congregation. Simple systems can ensure that names are recalled in church around the anniversary of deaths, that sick lists are up to date and, where appropriate, birthdays are remembered. The fear of forgetting people can be an excuse for not naming people. A parish priest I knew of would not allow names of the sick to be prayed for during the Sunday intercessions because someone might be forgotten and feel excluded. Yet this was deeply painful for regular members of the congregation when, for instance, a sick husband was being named in the intercessions in churches across the country but not in his own. People might be missed but it is probably important to have a mechanism which alerts the priest to the fact that they have been forgotten or were not known!

As a curate I carelessly lost a piece of paper on which someone had written a name for the All Souls' service; she came and the name was not read out. Her tears at the end alerted us to a problem. I had to apologize and then learn from her that this name was a child who had died and whom she had not really talked about. My poor administration had hurt her; however, I was able to apologize and find a way to remember the child and honour her loss. The experience has stayed with me because it taught me that paperwork matters: it is connected to people.

The Bishop of St Albans, John Taylor, used to write to all the clergy of a parish the week before that parish came up in the cycle of prayer. The letter asked whether they had any special requests for prayer but said, 'If not, please be assured the Bishop will be praying for you and your ministry on that day.' The letters would have been generated by an efficient secretary, but we knew that the Bishop would be praying and that felt affirming. One priest asked him if he felt bogged down in all the administration and he responded by saying that the administration is pastoral care: it is all about the people. For those like me who struggle with paperwork and organized systems, this is a key point to remember: good administration can help us cherish people. Systems that enable us to remember names and details of people's individual stories, that flag up important anniversaries in people's lives, can all help us to find ways of affirming and valuing the people God has gifted to our care.

In cherishing people in the community of the church and the wider parish, clergy are engaged in developing relations which are continuing and long term. In these relationships there is the luxury of attending to people over time. We are able to see them in different settings, listen to their stories, watch them with others and develop a genuine relationship. This means that time spent in visiting, sharing in social events and encouraging participation in different aspects of ministry is all immensely valuable. Such opportunities allow us simply to chat to people or engage in what one clergyman calls 'mooching' – simply taking time to hear people's joys and grumbles. It is in these kinds of encounters that we get to know each other. Such chatting may appear to be incidental to the 'real' work of parish ministry, but I suggest it is a vital aspect of developing and building up community life. Through ordinary human encounters individuals come to know the vicar better and the vicar gets to know them. Thus false expectations and inappropriate fears or fantasies can be assuaged, leading to more mutually affirming patterns of relating.

One of the strengths of parish ministry is that clergy live in the parish. That is, they live among those they are caring for; the same streets are local, they bump into people in the shops or while walking the dog. They may have children at the same school or attend the same fitness class or football matches. Thus the vicar becomes a multifaceted person. She is the vicar but she is also the owner of the hairy dog, the mother of those children, the one who gets worked up when her team loses and the one who sometimes runs out of bread or coffee and has to rush out to the shops. She is human. Equally the vicar sees people as multifaceted, encountering them in different aspects of their lives. This is different from many other caring professions, where people are only met in one situation. It is this recognition of the complexity of each individual that should help clergy and parishioners to treat each other as unique subjects rather than types.

Attending to the stranger

Parish clergy, as well as developing attentive sustaining relationships with the congregation and those regularly encountered in the wider parish, need to attend well in fleeting relationships. Occasional offices and particular parish events mean that clergy become involved in the lives of individuals at moments where they may be vulnerable. A frequent occurrence for most clergy is meeting people for the first time in a state of bereavement. Clergy therefore need to develop the skill of attending to people and situations very quickly. The practice they have in attending to those they know over time will help hone the skills necessary for this quick reading of people and circumstances. On entering a room a priest needs to communicate through her body language and through her conversation that she is focusing on these people, that she recognizes the unique reality of their loss. She will have visited many similar people in similar situations but never one that is the same as this family grieving this particular loss. Ruddick writes:

Attention is akin to the capacity for empathy, the ability to suffer or celebrate with another as if in the other's experience you know and find yourself. However, the idea of empathy, as it is popularly understood, underestimates the importance of knowing another without finding yourself in her.[3]

In many pastoral encounters it is this kind of knowing that is required, the reality of knowing another who is different and going through emotions that may well be alien to the priest. It needs more than empathy: it needs compassion, the ability to recognize the suffering or joy of another and feel with that individual in it but not be caught up in it oneself. We note how in the Gospels Jesus has compassion for the crowd and for the sick. He recognizes their needs and responds to them appropriately.

Ruddick identifies compassion as a virtue. This virtue guards against an excess of detachment, which can become lack of interest or an inability to recognize suffering different from one's own. People will react to things in their own way and may feel distressed or upset over something to a level that seems excessive. To be compassionate is to recognize the depth of feeling even if we do not fully comprehend their reaction. It is to sympathize truly. Proper compassion also guards against the temptation to feel everything ourselves, over-identifying with another's suffering and losing the detachment which *is* necessary to be able to help. Such over-identifying can all too easily shift the focus from the one in need back on to the carer. Perspective is necessary in caring for people, and I will look in more detail at this when discussing comforting in the next chapter. In attending to these people in these situations, in practising realism and compassion, a priest is also engaged in prayer. Attending to God in these situations is an essential aspect of how a priest can cherish these people and is something to which I return at the end of the chapter.

Concrete thinking – contextualizing

To read people well is a skill that can be developed through the practice of ministry. It involves paying attention to the non-verbal messages; reading body language and taking note of the setting and circumstances. On entering a room for a pastoral visit, good clergy, almost without thinking, are picking up signs to help them focus on this situation. How distressed, nervous, angry or uncomfortable is she? Are we perching uncomfortably in the best room or in a space where she feels at home? Who else is around? Will they come in or hover in the kitchen? The priest will already have some context: this woman's husband has died. Now she collects more – had he been ill long, how long had they been married, is there family? All of these things help to contextualize this bereavement, enabling the priest to respond to this particular woman who has lost her husband after a long marriage and a short unexpected illness.

She is drawing on the experience she has of other bereavements and other women of similar age to find an appropriate way of responding to this woman, in this situation. Parish clergy do this in many different pastoral encounters: delighting in this baby who is central to the lives of this couple, listening to the account of this illness specific to this man, and preparing a wedding for these two people and their unique relationship. The multiplicity of different encounters in similar situations can and should help in responding well in this one, but the process of understanding the uniqueness of *this* is necessary for the people to feel attended to, recognized and cared for. In these occasional encounters, the ability to recognize and value people, to cherish and care for them for the duration of a particular situation, bears witness to the care and concern that God has for each person. Ordained clergy represent God and the Church so the ability to attend well, to be present to them and to treat these people as unique individuals going through a specific set of experiences, can make concrete for them the grace and love of God.

Sometimes such ministry will bear fruit that we can see developing into a continuing relationship. A funeral done well may bring someone into the life of the church; a baptism in which the family felt valued and affirmed may encourage them to come to church more often. Sometimes the fruit becomes apparent years down the line, but in many cases trust is needed that this ministry is valued by God even if there is no obvious return. Sadly, in my ministry I have encountered individuals who have not felt cherished by the Church: those who in seeking the baptism of their child felt treated like a type with hoops to jump through and no one listening to their story; those who sat through funerals of loved ones that felt rushed and unconnected to the one they had lost. Failures to attend properly to those who turn to the Church for affirmation at times of difficulty or joy can leave lasting wounds which make it difficult for people to hear about God's love for them.

In saying this I am not unaware of the tensions inherent in the role. As discussed in the previous chapter, the call to preserve faith, however fragile, can be in tension with the call to challenge growth and to set out the boundaries of what Christianity is. Different situations may lead to a prioritizing of one over the other, and the theological understanding of a particular congregation will of course play a part in this. Thus, for instance, some parishes will prioritize teaching to ensure that those who seek baptism are committed Christians. Yet when this desire to prepare people properly turns into a one-size-fits-all response to all enquiries, important pastoral encounters can be mishandled.

The area in Sheffield where I was working had a high percentage of older mothers, and a number of the babies born were after IVF and other fertility treatments. These couples needed to have their struggles and joys recognized. When they encountered well-meaning churches which told them that before they could discuss baptism of this much-wanted child they needed to come to church for a certain number of meetings, they felt treated as cases, not individuals. They felt that their own struggles and joys were unimportant to the church and, by extension, to God. Whatever the parish policy, an early visit in which the story of this new life is properly listened to, and issues in the family understood, is necessary so that they know they have been recognized as individuals, not treated as types.

Sue Gerhardt, who writes about infant development, calls this 'contingent responsiveness'. She has this to say about how adults, as well as babies, are looking for a response which recognizes the concrete reality of who they are and what they are going through:

> Each baby needs a tailor-made response, not an off-the-shelf kind, however benign . . . If you think of your own experience as an adult, you become aware that you too need contingent response. General 'niceness', such as people being 'kind' when you are upset in some way, can be quite useless . . . What works much better is to feel other people willing to get on your wavelength – understanding the specific way that you are feeling, helping you to express it, and thinking about solutions with you.[4]

Contingent responsiveness requires concrete thinking; it means that people and their needs must be contextualized.

In preparation for ministry, in continuing training, reading and diocesan or wider church initiatives, we are often given generic models for being and growing church. These abstract ideas can be useful for stimulating our thinking but they always need to be adapted to the reality of this place and these people. When my first child settled quickly into a good rhythm of feeding, the midwife jokingly said, 'I see you got one that had read the book.' What she meant was that there was some kind of luck if your child behaved like the child in the literature, which is, of course, by definition a fantasy child. The danger is that we may assume the child will then continue to behave just like the book and will become frustrated with ourselves or the child if he does not. The same is true for people, places and parishes.

It takes time and effort to respond to real people in this way, to attend properly to the long-term relationships and the fleeting encounters so that people feel recognized, heard and cherished. Attending lovingly to people is, as Ruddick suggests, a discipline and a virtue. Many clergy are drawn into parish ministry because they already have a developed capacity for attentively caring for people. Although it is undoubtedly true that such attending comes more easily to some than others, the notion that it is a discipline and a virtue helps us to see that it can be learnt, honed and developed. Like all such virtues it is developed through practice. The more we attend lovingly to people, the better at it we become. The more honestly we can reflect on our failures to cherish people or see them as gifts, the greater will be our chance of improving our capacity to attend.

Contextual ministry – attending to this place

In the discussion above I have focused on the way that priests need to attend to the reality of individuals in continuing and fleeting encounters. Yet as well as caring for many individuals the parish priest has to have a concept of caring for this or these parishes as a whole. Parishes have characters and they have stories. Just as it is important to recognize the uniqueness of each person and not treat them as types, so priests have to understand the uniqueness of the community as a whole and its setting.

On arriving in a parish a priest needs to attend to it, learning its unique character. It may be that the parish is physically like the place where she served her curacy. It has the same mix of housing and a similar population size. Like the last place it is on the edge of a bigger city with lots of commuters, a good school and a handful of local shops. Yet this is unlikely to mean that the two parishes function in exactly the same way. Each will have a unique history. The clergy who have gone before in this place will be different from the ones in the previous parish. The dynamics of relationships within the congregation will be different, shaped by the particular personalities who have been around for a long time. The relationship between the church and the wider parish can turn on particular events which are perceived to have been handled well or badly. If the priest assumes that this is pretty much the same parish as her curacy, she may well assume that the same things will work and be deeply disappointed when they do not.

As we noted at the start of this chapter, attending properly means letting go of the fantasy or fears we project on to people and communities. In mothering, Ruddick suggests that realism is a virtue. This virtue in ministry means having a clear-sighted vision of the reality of a place and its situation. The temptations Ruddick suggests result from an over-editing of the facts, which leads to a cheery denial of problems, or a pessimistic depression, which leads to a lack of hope for the place. To avoid trying to minister to the fantasy parish, clergy need to find constructive ways of attuning themselves to the reality of *this* parish. This requires concrete thinking and a proper understanding of the context of this place. It means knowing its history as well as its geography and own sense of identity.

We have a number of friends who have adopted children at various ages, and moving into a new parish has similarities to the task of mothering a child who has not been in your family from birth. Many come with a complex history of past relationships which need to be understood for the benefit of this new relationship. In parish ministry we are always following someone else. It can be demoralizing for an incoming priest to be told that the last vicar was particularly good at things she knows are her weak points. It can also be bewildering when people react to suggestions a new vicar makes in surprising ways because they are assuming that you are just like your predecessor. My relationship with an organist in the parish was made more complicated for both of us because he consistently feared that I was going to change the church music in a similar way to a previous vicar he worked with. I could not have been more unlike that vicar and my agenda for the music was very different, but in his eyes all vicars who changed things were in a sense one type.

Understanding the good and bad of past relationships is helpful for establishing trust and development in the new relationship. Where congregations and parishes have felt neglected or abused by previous incumbents, diocesan re-ordering decisions or wider social events, then time and effort will be needed to rebuild trust. Reactions to everyday situations and expectations may be unpredictable and challenging. It helps to know what has gone on before. In the process of learning about the story of the parish a priest must be realistic, acknowledging the difficult as well as the good, but also compassionate. Ideally the new parish will have been lovingly cared for in the past, but even so there is often some residual sense of abandonment that the last person left, even if that leaving was expected and the move to new things celebrated. And it can be hard to follow someone who is constantly held up as the perfect vicar.

The attending to the past of a parish involves listening to the myriad stories and piecing together a picture of its history. It is not just recent history that shapes the particular character of a place. Where and when a church was built can often reflect issues from past generations which, like family history, have some bearing on the life of that parish today. Is this a once wealthy community which has fallen on hard times? How does this parish relate to the one down the hill or in the next village? There can be residual tension about a daughter church which has seemed to eclipse its mother, or a church which once stood in the heart of a village only to find the village has moved in the other direction. Local history and census information can help in contextualizing the place. It can also sometimes help in ensuring that the stories told are grounded in reality. Perceptions about demographics may not fit the real picture. A colleague used to talk about the parish he cared for as predominantly Muslim; actually this group was just shy of 10 per cent of the population, but they had changed the make-up of the High Street. Both the perception – this community has changed and now looks and feels different – and the reality – it is less mixed than you think – need to be reflected on to understand the place.

Storytelling

In bringing up children we help to situate them in their own story by telling the stories of the family they belong to, narrating the lives of the parents, grandparents and their early years, as well as the stories of the community in which they are living. At its best this understanding of a past is a helpful way of encouraging growth and development into the future; it expresses that life is a changing unfolding story in which we all play our part. It teaches the importance of contextualizing life; who we are is shaped by where we come from and who we come from, not in a way that necessarily binds us but in a way that affects us. Parish clergy need to be good at listening to stories and at telling them. The Ordinal calls on priests to 'tell the story of God's love' and that story needs to be told in a way that connects to the reality of these people and this place. Aspects of God's story that are comforting in one community may be deeply challenging for another. What is important is to find ways of narrating the story of this place that are realistic, compassionate and also hopeful.

Narrating the history of a church building or given community can give people the perspective of time and perhaps help them understand how to look forward to the future. Holy Trinity, Millhouses, was a relatively new building from the 1930s, but it was good to learn that the route taken by the monks of Beauchief Abbey, to pray at the chapel on the hill at Ecclesall, had been straight through what was now Holy Trinity parish. Our history was connected to the prayerful life of the past, and this could help us think about our role as a prayerful place now and in the future. Knowing when and why a church was built, what the vision was then, can help make sense of strange geography and connect us to the faith of our forebears. Understanding the past can help us realize that we have a part to play in continuing the story of faith in this place for the now and into the future.

Anglican parishes live with the complexity of previous ideas about mission, and it is important that we understand them in getting to know who we are now. Knowing something of how and why our buildings are as they are and where they are can help us in trying to love and appreciate even the unwieldy and unlovely. Whatever Christians may think about the reality of the church as people, not buildings, the wider population find it harder to distinguish the two. It is buildings that people recognize as pointers to the Christian faith and they have significance for the wider community. Realism and compassion may also help address the difficult histories and the possibility that some loved church buildings may no longer be in the right place or configured in the right way.

Understanding the history prevents the implementation of short-term changes with no thought for how things might be used in the future. It can also help us change perceptions where communities have developed a narrative of being unimportant, forgotten or unsuccessful. Parents can sometimes stifle a child's abilities by unfavourably comparing him to others or showing little interest in his particular talents. So too churches can misnarrate their story by inappropriate comparisons or a fixation on the wrong criteria for success. I will return to these issues in Chapter 8.

Things change

As well as learning the long-term history of a parish church, there needs to be time spent learning the more recent history of relationships within it. A new parish priest needs to learn, sensitively, more about what has happened in recent years. Parishes are not static, and however long one has been in a place things will be changing and hopefully growing, so the history is an unfolding story. Not only do we need to take seriously the reality that all people are unique and therefore need to be recognized for themselves rather than as types, but we also need to acknowledge that people are constantly changing.

In the mother–child relationship this is obvious because change is relatively rapid and what was appropriate for a two-year-old may be inappropriate for a five-year-old. Thus constantly adapting to and rereading one's children is an important aspect of mothering. In ministry the sense of growing and changing needs to be understood most profoundly in the relationship with the community as a whole. Parishes change as those involved become more mature in age and faith, as new people join and others die or move away. Most clergy will at some points in their ministry be confronted with someone telling them that 'We tried that once and it didn't work'. Recognizing that congregations and communities grow and change can help clergy to respond appropriately, suggesting that now is not then and helping those within to recognize their own journeys of growth.

In contextualizing the reality of people and places, we invite them to tell their stories. Sometimes all that is needed is a good listening ear. However, often help is needed for people and communities to tell their stories and hear how their own story fits into the wider stories of those around them and into the continuing story of God's involvement in the world.[5] Thus clergy need to be good at listening to, interpreting and telling stories. In order for these stories to be helpful, clergy need to think reflectively and to help others to do so. They have to be able to think imaginatively so that they can explore ways of moving forward, perhaps renarrating this history in a more hopeful way.

If a particular congregation feel marginalized by history and have had a succession of clergy who have only stayed for a short time, then it will not be surprising if they are mistrustful of new initiatives. If the new vicar brings her own history of insecurities she may misread their fears as personal criticism of her ideas and become either defensive or disillusioned. Where there is good reflective thinking then these reactions can be narrated differently. An acknowledgement of the way the congregation feels it has been let down by others can allow a proper discussion about their fears and how they can rebuild trust in the wider Church and God. The vicar may admit her own lack of expertise while offering the reality of her commitment and desire to work with them for a more constructive future. Proper attention and good reflective thinking allows genuine trust to develop through an honest acknowledgement of hurts and failures.

Learning reflective thinking through chatting

There is a tendency to assume that reflective thinking is something that we do on our own: a kind of contemplative going over things. This is of course a valuable aspect of reflection. However, if, as I suggest above, we are reflecting on both our own fears and fantasies and those of others, we may in our heads simply deepen our misreadings of a situation. Ruddick suggests that in mothering, reflective thinking is developed and honed through conversations: through the kind of chatting that may well be dismissed as idle talk. This is an extremely valuable insight which can help us in thinking about developing reflective thinking in the practice of ministry. So what does Ruddick mean?

She suggests that it is through chatting to others who share a similar practice, telling stories about our children and the experience of caring for them, that we learn to judge and rethink our own way of doing things.

> In their storytelling, mothers share and elaborate their observations, making a coherent, often amusing, dramatic, or poignant story of their children's particularities. Individually and collectively, they rehearse their judgements and establish continuities in their ongoing nurturing activities.[6]

In my own experience of mothering there have been three main constituencies with whom I have had these kinds of conversations about the children. Such conversations have sometimes been deliberately initiated, but much of the time they just happen. This chatting has helped me reflect on my practice, honing my ability to attend well and respond appropriately to the changing lives of my particular boys.

First, there have been frequent conversations with those who have shared in the care for the children and who, like me, are deeply invested in their future well-being. Principally this has involved endless conversations with their father, where we narrate the daily lives of the children and reflect together on how they are, where they are going and how we are to be with and for them. It has also at different stages of their life involved conversations with nannies who took on much of the daily routine of their lives and other close friends and family members who love the boys and have been able to help me reflect on the process of bringing them up.

The second group are those who are themselves bringing up children: mothers chatting about their children to other mothers. Their children are different, but in sharing the stories of success, failure, confusion and delight, in caring for our particular children, we have been able to challenge, comfort, reassure and inspire each other in the continuing practice of bringing up children. Ruddick in her book worries that this may be a dying art as changing patterns of women's work create less obvious spaces for such chattering, but its very importance has led women to find new ways of doing it, hence the development of virtual networks where these conversations happen in a new way.

The third group of conversation partners are the children themselves. As they have grown and developed, the ways in which such conversations happen have altered but there have always, even when their capacity to reason was more limited, been opportunities to reflect together on how our behaviour impacts on each other. The chatty conversations have helped to enable the children to understand their history, to place themselves within a narrative that is both historical and cultural. It has enabled us to explore fears and fantasies, to question each other's responses where they seem inappropriate and renegotiate the relationship as age and experience requires. We have explored tricky issues of dependence and independence at so many levels, what it means to love and be loved and how we should behave towards others.

These kinds of continuing conversations have been vital in helping me reflect on my role as a mother. At times they have helped change the way I do things and encouraged me to try out new strategies and to have different expectations. At times they have helped me to be kinder to myself and or kinder to the children. This is a continuing process. Recently a difficult decision about changing my younger son's schooling involved me in endless conversations with him, with those who know him and love him, with other mothers and other educators. These conversations helped me to reflect on my own fears and fantasies, critique some of my assumptions and continually focus myself back on to the question, 'What is the best thing for this particular child, at this particular stage of his life, in these circumstances?' It was a process of collective reflective thinking which helped all of us, including my son, feel that we had made the right decision, which experience has confirmed.

Ruddick suggests that all of these conversations need to be shaped by the virtues of realism, compassion and delight. In the discussions above, realism and compassion have already been identified and I will discuss delight in more detail in the next chapter. Here, I note how Ruddick connects them to storytelling and conversational reflection. She suggests that we are tempted to over-edit our accounts, cutting out the difficult bits. Alternatively, in failing to edit we end up sharing more than is appropriate and kind. Over-editing often means that we fail to tackle the more complex feelings and experiences by trying to make ourselves or our children appear better than we are, presenting in fact a fantasy.

In speaking truthfully about our own or others' children and in commenting on our own and others' practice, we need to be compassionate, avoiding sarcasm or unfeeling critiques, while being able to address sympathetically what is inappropriate. Honesty, tempered with kindness, is needed in telling, listening to and interpreting our own and others' stories. Ruddick suggests that the virtue of delight is needed to guard against the temptation to perfectionism and competitiveness as well as the more obvious dismissal of things we ourselves find uninteresting. These temptations are all recognizable. As Ruddick says, to name the virtues is not necessarily to possess them but to understand the temptations better so that we can improve the practice.

Learning through conversation in ministry

In parish ministry the development of reflective thinking can be developed through valuing this same kind of conversational story-telling. The conversation partners should include those who share responsibility and concern for this parish: the other clergy, ministers and office holders with responsibilities for these people and this place. Conversations are also needed with those engaged in similar responsibility for different people and places. These conversations should provide opportunities to talk undefensively about the realities of ministry in ways that can encourage the sharing of good practice, the compassionate critique of mistakes and the wisdom that can come from a different person's insight into a continuing situation.

The conversations need to be realistic but compassionate. They do not need to be heavily engineered moments of deep analysis; instead, it is important to find ways in which these conversations can feel ordinary and unforced, a chatting about the daily ups and downs of parish ministry which can be all too rare in our isolated models of parochial care. In my first incumbency I was blessed by the presence of a retired bishop in the congregation. He joined me most days for evening prayer and we would chat about the life of the church. His compassionate insights could at times gently critique my unintentional misreadings of people, while at other times his reassurance could help me stay strong through a tricky situation. I also benefited from regular meetings with other clergy, where I found it possible to talk through my experiences openly, knowing I was being carefully listened to.

For most priests, organizing groups where it feels safe to chat through the ups and downs of parish life takes time and energy, yet such groups can be invaluable in sustaining a proper perspective on parish life. There are organized local events such as deanery chapter or local ecumenical clergy gatherings. Sometimes these work well, but too often the concerns of competitiveness and insecurity mean that the chatting involves only heavily edited stories. Particular churchmanship or special interests can facilitate the forming of groups in which people may find it easier to be honest with each other. However, these need to guard against a tendency to reinforce certain outlooks in ways that militate against a realistic assessment of ministerial life.

The historical patterns of parish ministry which have encouraged an isolated role for the parish priest are problematic for this kind of reflective thinking. We need to encourage and develop many opportunities for clergy to meet with fellow clergy, those they are similar to and those very different, where in incidental chatting stories of parish ministry can be told, listened to, reflected on and learnt from. Many of us would agree that at conferences the most valuable things learnt are often in the conversations had over lunch, coffee or a few drinks in the bar.

Even if a parish priest is isolated from other clergy her role is always a social one as she relates to all of the different people within the parish. Here she needs to develop the kind of reflective conversations that enable the community to think about who they are, what they are doing and how they are doing it. The community has a wonderful mix of perspectives to bring to these conversations. There are individuals who have a long history in this place and those who can see it with the eyes of newcomers. There are people who have insights from many different professions outside the church and who can raise questions of good practice from other walks of life. It is hoped that there are young and old, male and female, people who live in families, alone or in different kinds of relationships. Some of these people will have a long-standing Christian faith; some will be theologically literate, some deeply prayerful, some challengingly prophetic.

These conversations are a form of theological reflection. As St Paul suggests, like a body the community will be made up of different parts with different gifts and competencies. Facilitating the conversations within a congregation and a wider parish needs the virtues of humility, realism and compassion. In talking about human interaction

Arendt reminds us that the process is not one in which the outcomes can be managed. Human interaction is creative; out of our conversations should come something new, the possibilities of new insights, new ways of doing things and a renewed sense of what it is to be in relationship with each other.

One of the ways that such conversations happen in a parish is through good opportunities for visiting and for social interactions. It is in the times we relax with each other that we can tell appropriate stories about what matters in our lives and in the continuing life of the community. Such time spent chatting can feel unproductive but it builds up the sense of relationship and develops the capacity to reflect together on the things that matter. It is time well spent. Incidental conversations can often highlight needs and tensions which can then be addressed in more intentional conversations.

Intentional conversations are necessary between individuals but also important for the whole church to reflect on how things are organized, prioritized and achieved. These too need to be open conversations. Yet because we cannot control the outcomes, such open conversations can feel risky for clergy who have a sense of responsibility for all those involved. It can therefore be a temptation to resist conversations about things that really matter as a way of avoiding conflict. As noted in the first chapter, an emphasis on particular targets and goals can suggest that prolonged conversations are a distraction from achieving the specified aims. Yet Arendt notes that it is only in a work model that the ends justify the means. When building up community and encouraging the growth of a church, the process matters. The church belongs to all its members and thus its activities need to be understood from as many perspectives as possible.

In Holy Trinity, when we decided to think about the policy of admitting children to Holy Communion before confirmation, we felt that the discussion process was vitally important. Some people suggested that as the vicar I should simply make a statement and decide on a policy. However, I knew that we needed to work this out together, and I as much as anyone else needed not just to hear the different arguments but to feel them. So over a year we had open meetings. Some of these looked at theological ideas around communion, the place of children and what it meant to be an inclusive church. Other meetings allowed a respectful sharing of feelings.

These often involved people telling their own stories, sharing fears and expectations. Through this process we agreed on how we would make a decision and then how the decision would be implemented. In all this we took seriously the fears expressed and a growing consensus about where we should be going as a church. When we arrived at implementing our decision not everyone agreed, but everyone knew they had been listened to and respected the process by which we had got there. Through the process unexpected issues arose that shed light on particular individuals' relationship to the church, enabling opportunities to heal past hurts and rethink attitudes, not just to children but to others who had felt excluded. It took time and the end result was not a given.

Attending to God

For priests, all the attending to people and places involves both a proper focusing on the concrete realities of now and a simultaneous focus on the eternal values of the kingdom of God. As a priest attends to people and places so she is also attending to God. What does God want for them? How does God want her to care for them, speak to them and learn from them? How does all of this everyday stuff fit into the coming of the kingdom? This means that in attending well to people and places clergy have a final vitally important conversation partner and that is God. Thus central to a reflective ministry is prayer.

The responsibility for the parish is taken on in partnership with God, who cares for these people and this place far more than we can imagine. God also knows and understands them and their place in the unfolding history of salvation. Prayer will be different to different people and different aspects of praying will be present in parish ministry. There will be formal prayers, which bookend the days and weeks, as well as the many informal moments of tuning in to God before, or as, we listen to or speak to others. Attention, I suggested earlier, is a form of attunement. Prayer is about the many different ways that we attune ourselves to God. Allowing space to converse with God about the people and situations we encounter enables us to reflect on how our understanding and our practice is in tune with God's values. It helps us to see them as gifts, to wrestle with what we find difficult about them and to ask for grace to love them as God does. Time spent attending to God should strengthen the sense that we are cherished by God, forgiven for our failings and refreshed for all that needs to be done. Prayer helps to focus on the broader vision, accepting that we do not know or understand the whole but can trust in God's loving purposes.

It is assumed that a priest will pray, and this double vision, this commitment to earthly realities alongside eternal hopes, is one of the activities people expect of a priest. In pastoral encounters the perspective which comes from being able to focus on the here and now while simultaneously attending to God and eternal truths is a particular gift that priests bring to their work. In my experience many individuals who are not minded to pray themselves, who are reasonably sure that there is no point in praying, still want to know that a priest is praying for them. As with all attention, attending to God in prayer and study is a discipline which takes time and energy. The more we practise the easier it becomes. The more we tune in to God the better we are able to draw on his grace to help in attuning to people and places.

In relating to parishes and the people within them, clergy need to take seriously the uniqueness of each individual and each place. They are called to cherish people and recognize that the rich and sometimes frustrating mix of individuals is God's gift for the ministry in this place. Not only are these people all individuals but they are also constantly changing, as people's life situations evolve, as people join and leave the community and as wider events impact on the life of this place. This means that clergy need to develop the capacity to attend continually and properly to the reality of these people, this place. They need reflective conversations to help them to think and reflect on the continuing life of the church.

Their care for the parish needs to be compassionate and the attention required needs to be understood as a virtue as well as a discipline. Through practice we should get better at it until attending well in one-off encounters and continuing relationships comes almost naturally. Failure to attend to the reality of the other leads us to objectify people as types on whom we project our fears and fantasies. We then meet the needs we expect them to have rather than listen to the reality of who they are and what their genuine need is. There is also the danger that in misreading people and situations through failure in attention, clergy may be over-ready to blame themselves for failures that are systemic or to blame others inappropriately. The responsibility to care and to bear witness to the Church's ministry of care can feel overwhelming at times, so it is vitally important that clergy have the people and places where they can chat undefensively and where they can rest on the attentive love of others. Central to their conversation partners needs to be the God who has called them to this place, who cherishes them and the people they care for.

4

Dependence and interdependence

————◆·●·◆————

Talking about ministry as being like mothering inevitably raises questions about dependency. Does imaging the priest as a mother inevitably mean that the congregation are seen as children? Is this simply a feminized version of 'Father knows best'? These questions are important for both mothering and ministry. Both practices need to think hard about questions of dependence, independence and interdependence. Within my household there are constant tensions around these issues: mini power struggles. With children who are adult and nearly adult but still dependent on their parents financially and in many other ways, it is not surprising to find that disagreements arise around levels of accountability and responsibility. Why should my adult son tell me if his plans change and he decides to stay over at friends'? My response to this is to stress the relationship we have: he should tell me because I care and he owes it to me to communicate enough for me to stop worrying!

Bringing up children has been, and continues to be, a process of negotiating, allowing space for independent explorations while being expected to be dependable whenever I am needed. The levels of independence and dependence have shifted and changed but the continuing relationship means that the children and I continue to expect things from each other. I have certain powers, particularly financial ones at the moment, and I need to be careful not to use them manipulatively. They have an expectation that I will be there for them whenever they need me. My role as mother still means that they can and do presume on my care for them.

Language about dependence and independence is connected to ideas about becoming adult. Maturity is assumed to mean independence and autonomy. Being dependent is often portrayed as a weakness and an inadequacy. These assumptions are important to think about in terms of parish ministry because priests are called to challenge the presumption that autonomy is the height of human maturity. Central to the Christian faith is the fact that we are all dependent on God, acknowledging that dependency is the beginning of developing a mature faith. Alongside this central truth is the social nature of Christianity. We are called to be interdependent on each other, living and working as a community of mutual care and responsibility. If collaborative ministry is the appropriate way of working in the church, it requires careful negotiations between people, relying on others and trusting them. This involves acknowledging the power inherent in relationships, especially when that power is unequally distributed.

This chapter will explore some of the complexities around power, dependency and trust. I will briefly look at the influence of Freudian concepts of child development, particularly the emphasis on separation from the mother as a necessity of an independent self. If, instead of valuing separation, mutuality is stressed, then it is possible to think more coherently about how children and adults move between periods of dependence, independence and interdependence. Many adult relationships involve appropriate levels of dependency and need to negotiate the power that is therefore present. Parish clergy in their formal and pastoral roles find themselves in a position of power, where others are dependent on them. I will look at the importance of understanding this dependence as transitional. I will also look at how power can be understood generatively and why trust and forgiveness are essential for this. Both mothers and priests find it difficult to talk about power within a relationship which is based on loving care, but failure to address these issues can lead to unintentional power games which are signs of immaturity and lack of mutuality.

Dependency and maturity

It is clear that a baby is dependent on someone older to care for him. A human child is extremely limited in his capacity to do anything to meet his own needs. He develops over the months and years, gradually acquiring more physical movement and dexterity so that he can begin to do things for himself. Alongside this physical development, which is a linear progression from a vulnerable infant to a fully matured man, is the mental and emotional process of developing a sense of self and the maturity we attach to adulthood. In this process of development the importance of independence is valued and often seen as the ultimate goal. Clearly, independence in looking after oneself is important. It is right to encourage a child to learn to dress, wash and feed himself. We do expect and want him to develop the capacity to make decisions and have appropriate control over his own actions. A large part of what mothers do is to facilitate this growing independence.

However, it does become more problematic when maturity is associated with emotional autonomy. Sigmund Freud's theory of the emotional development of the self continues to influence the way a child's progression towards adulthood is understood. This is not the place to go into great detail and I am aware that what I write here is a simplification. In Freudian theory a child needs to move from a sense of merged identity with the mother, rejecting the maternal world, and moving into the more autonomous world of the father. This has characterized growing up and maturity as a process of separation. The child distances himself from the mother and her world of care. It is interesting to note how this feeds into popular understanding so that those, especially boys, who have not done this are criticized as 'mummy's boys', 'tied to the apron strings', with the implication that they are immature.

This underlying presumption that maturity comes from leaving the mother has also led to the portrayal of mothers as those who resist their child's independence. Growing up is thus understood as a kind of power struggle as the child tries to break free of the 'smothering' care of his mother. Mothers may be characterized as those who use their power, often manipulatively, to keep their children dependent, who do not want to see their children grow up because that involves their growing away. Clearly, we can find enough experiential truth in this for it to be part of the popular caricature of mothers.

Yet I would suggest that it is an inaccurate caricature, one that describes a serious temptation for mothers but not a realistic picture of the patterns of power, dependency and interdependency present in most experiences of growing up. Freud's theories have been critiqued by those who suggest that he has misunderstood the mother–child relationship from the outset. The writer Bonnie Miller-McLemore states

> Human growth does not involve a movement from dependence to independence. Rather, growth entails learning more and more sophisticated modes of relating, with a movement from immature dependencies to more mature dependencies and attachments.[1]

In saying this she, like others, maintains that from the beginning the mother and child are recognizably two separate subjects who have to negotiate how to be together. The child is dependent on the mother for his care, but it is clear to the mother that he is an independent personality who, as we noted in the previous chapter, she has to learn to know.

This is about relationship: a relationship between two subjects who bring different levels of dependency and power but who are, at best, seeking mutuality. Jessica Benjamin writes at length about this in *The Bonds of Love*.

> Although the baby is wholly dependent upon her – and not only on her, but perhaps equally on a father or others – never for a moment does she doubt that this baby brings his own self, his unique personality, to bear on their common life. And she is grateful for the baby's cooperation and activity.[2]

Here we see that although this is at one level an unequal relationship – the baby is wholly dependent on her – it is also a relationship in which both are active. As the child develops physically and mentally, learning how to do things himself, so the relationship continues to aim for cooperation. As Miller-McLemore says, it moves into more and more sophisticated patterns of interdependence and collaboration.

In this relationship the child's development and growth is celebrated. A mother proudly delights in her child's first steps. On the one hand they make the child more independent, but they also mean that he needs his mother to assess risks differently, to renegotiate the way that they move around together and to think for him about how to utilize this skill safely; this involves the cooperation that Benjamin mentions above. The process of moving around is adapted to make the interdependence of the two work together. Clearly the mother still has considerable power over this relationship. She can use it to pick the child up physically or to restrict his movement by gates and fences. He also has power: he can scream and shout, make his body rigid and resist his mother's efforts to curb his movements. But if the two individuals want to be in a relationship of mutuality, they find ways of constructively managing this newfound freedom. The child accepts some limitations and trusts that when all this running around has got too much he can ask to be carried. Children oscillate between periods of independence and periods of dependency, and this is healthy. Mothers and children are constantly negotiating and at best collaborating as children move towards maturity.

The aim of bringing up children is that they will become independent in many aspects of their life so that they can be confident adults. Yet to equate adulthood with autonomy and assume that independence is always the goal is to misunderstand the social and relational nature of human beings. The model of an entirely independent adult is a caricature, and not a particularly healthy one. We are social creatures and we need relationships of interdependence and mutual dependency. We seek this in friendships and marriage, where we talk about the importance of being able to depend on others. Most of us acknowledge that there are times in life when we feel vulnerable and we long for another, whom we trust, to care for us and support us. We feel the need metaphorically to be carried or held, just for a while. Thus as mature adults we continue to oscillate between periods of independence and times when we are willingly dependent on others.

Yet saying this implies that such dependence is always a choice. The reality is that as adults we encounter many relationships where we are dependent on others, not through a mutually loving relationship but through the ordinary and extraordinary events of living in a world of other human beings. We experience the daily limitations of being dependent on the people at the till to process our shopping, the receptionist to access the doctor, the doctor to access treatment we need, and so on. Within our workplace we are dependent on others to do their jobs properly in order for us to do our own. These can offer us good models of interdependence or destructive models of power games, frustrations and at worst conflict.

Dependency in the church

Central to the Christian faith is the underlying belief that we are always dependent on God. This is why religion is often dismissed as a weakness: it invites adults to admit to their dependency. The gathering together for worship is a time to focus on this dependency, which underpins all of life. Our dependence on God is significantly different from our dependence on other people. It is a fact of our existence which we can choose to acknowledge or not. In acknowledging this truth we explore the relationship in terms analogous to our experience of other relationships. Thus we talk about coming into God's presence, of drawing close to God and seeking at times a sense of resting in dependence, as if being held by the love of the perfect parent. Aspects of worship and of pastoral care make tangible this sense of being fed, held and nurtured by God. This tangibility is mediated through rituals and through those who represent God. Priests, through their ordination, have a particular responsibility for speaking and acting in God's name. Formally in word and sacrament and informally through the authority of their ordination, priests communicate the truths and grace of God to those for whom they have responsibility.

It therefore follows that people are dependent on a parish priest for aspects of ministry that sustain their faith. She is the gatekeeper for certain rituals and sacraments. Week by week members of the congregation are dependent on the priest's role in the liturgy absolving them, feeding them in word and sacrament and sending them out with God's blessing. New parents bringing their baby for baptism are dependent on the priest for the affirmation and blessing they are seeking. A couple applying to be married in the church are dependent on the priest for her legal and spiritual presence. She has a level of power in her relationships with others. Priests need to ensure that they are not using their power, in these rituals, in ways that place barriers between people and their access to the ministry of the church. It can be tempting to stress the priest's importance, focusing on her role rather than God's grace. She is there to facilitate their access to God and their ability to receive from him all they need for their life of dependence on him.

The church is the community where people learn about God revealed in Jesus Christ, where they find the resources they need to strengthen and deepen their faith. The parish priest has a primary responsibility for overseeing the teaching of the parish and how the Christian faith is understood both formally and informally. Many will have their understanding of God and of appropriate Christian discipleship shaped by the preaching and teaching offered in their particular church. The priest, to some extent, speaks in the name of God and therefore her theological understanding, her pronouncements and her behaviour shape people's picture of Christian beliefs and practice.

There is a level of dependency within the congregation which an individual priest needs to negotiate with care. What is she modelling, and what are they learning? How is it possible to encourage mature thinking which allows for different ideas and still provide a coherent message? As we saw in Ruddick's demands of mothering, there is an inherent tension between providing what is needed for people's preservation and security alongside their need for challenge and growth. There is also the demand, which she calls 'acceptability', training for social acceptance. The priest as the authorized minister for the church has a role in defining what is and is not acceptable. How this authority is exercised impacts on individuals and the wider community.

A young woman I know was asked to sign a large number of doctrinal statements before she could help with the children's work at her church. This particular church placed a great emphasis on conformity to the agreed doctrines, of which the incumbent was the final arbiter. There was one statement that this woman felt unable to sign because experiences of people she cared for had caused her to question the very strict line her church was advocating. The pastoral structures in this large church meant that her concerns were relayed up to the rector through a series of individuals – she could not simply arrange to see him herself. The eventual result was the issuing of a simple statement: if she could not sign, she could not help in the children's work, but at no point did any of the senior clergy offer to talk through the personal, pastoral and theological issues that she was dealing with.

Here the senior parish priest used his power to decide who could and who could not take on a role in the church. He also used it to decide who had access directly to him. In this instance, the use of power did not allow for cherishing an individual with genuine questions. The assumption was made that in questioning this issue she was de facto not suitable. In this church, acceptability in terms of doctrinal agreement was prioritized above this individual's preservation or growth. The power dynamics are clear: her ability to share in an aspect of the church's ministry was dependent on her conformity to the rector's understanding of acceptable Christian teaching.

The dynamics in smaller parishes will be different, but parish priests will still have a responsibility to weigh up the different demands of preserving faith, encouraging growth and training in acceptability. They have, through their role, the power to shape what is acceptable and who participates in debates about this acceptability. Thus parish priests may be tempted to limit debate and discourage critical discussions for a variety of reasons. The motivation may be driven by a valuing of their own training experience, or continuing training, which reassures them that in spiritual or theological matters they are the experts. They may then feel a duty to control the ideas explored within and beyond the church for fear that ignorance or 'wrong' teaching may lead people into error. They themselves may feel dependent on the approbation of others they look up to, or a particular understanding of God. This kind of thinking can lead to infantilizing the congregation and a mother- (or more likely a father-) knows-best model of ministry. However benignly meant, this is a form of domination which values obedience and conformity above mutuality and interdependence.

Yet a priest cannot simply let go of any responsibility for over-seeing the understanding of God and Christian doctrine which the Church teaches and embodies, any more than a mother can let go of protecting and training her child. Individuals are dependent on the Church for providing the environment in which they can learn and develop their discipleship. The temptation to neglect the difficult issues of faith, which might challenge people's behaviour, inevitably leads to a diminished vision of the gospel. A given church community will be saying things about God and Christianity explicitly or implicitly. Allowing people the space to explore faith and ask questions still requires a coherent presentation of the truths of the faith, even if they are allowed to be challenged.

In a community of interdependence and mutual learning, a priest has a duty to use her knowledge and training for the benefit of others. A stipendiary priest is someone who has been set free from other ways of earning a living to be able to focus her thinking and learning on how we know and relate to God as individuals and as a church. She has some level of expertise, which should be used to help develop everyone's maturity. She cannot neglect her duty to teach the boundaries of faith in a misguided belief that this frees people. She needs instead to share her knowledge and insights collaboratively to build up the whole, not to control all the outcomes.

Conscientiousness

In her writing about mothering, Ruddick talks about encouraging 'acceptability' in the context of training children in conscientiousness.

The mother, she suggests, seeks to develop a relationship of mutual trust with her child that allows them to develop their own conscientiousness, and she does this by being conscientious. She resists the temptation to require blind obedience to her values. Yet she also knows that she must communicate her values well, so that children have criteria for naming what is good and bad. Even in areas where they come to disagree with her values, she needs to have given them an appropriate methodology for arriving at their decision. Conscientiousness is a mark of maturity. Ruddick notes that we recognize such maturity in growing children when they behave well in situations which they have had to negotiate for themselves.

To be conscientious is not the same as being independent. It assumes that one's behaviour does impact on other people; it acknowledges the interdependence necessary for mature human interaction. For Christians such conscientiousness relates to the maturity envisioned when the New Testament talks about individuals growing up into Christ. They are to develop ways of thinking and acting as Christians, not out of a slavish adherence to law but through developing a Christian character. Tom Wright's book *Virtue Reborn* offers an in-depth study of these New Testament ideas about maturity and the development of virtue.[3]

So we can then conclude that the role of a parish priest means that in a general way people are dependent on her for access to the sacraments, for teaching and modelling the Christian life and overseeing appropriate discussions about the limits of good Christian behaviour and doctrine. To fulfil her role conscientiously she must find an appropriate balance between asserting her position as the only acceptable one and failing to provide the criteria by which people can assess their own and others' ideas. The kind of reflective learning through chatting described in the previous chapter is one of the ways conscientiousness is developed in priests and all people. A secure sense of self is also needed, so that a priest can deal constructively with challenges to her faith and her authority. For all of us, Christian faith is a journey, and issues which appeared to be clear cut at one stage of life may begin to look more complex at another stage. Continuing study, discussion and an openness to learn is necessary for a priest to resist the temptation to misuse her authority to stifle the growing faith of others.

Transitional dependency and generous inequality

Priests are uncomfortable in talking about the power and authority they have because it seems out of place in a community of mutuality and love. Yet they need to acknowledge that the role brings this authority, which is neutral. It is how it is used and how the relationships are valued that matters. Celia Allison Hahn's helpful book *Growing in Authority, Relinquishing Control* explores how to find collaborative ways of using the authority which comes with the role. When this does not happen, she writes:

> When authority really means control in church settings, a number of difficulties are set in motion. Leaders become more interested in being right than being helpful. Religious leaders who grab all the authority find themselves crushed by the burden of such a load of responsibility. They end up overloaded, resentful, and treading the burnout road. The lay people, on the other hand, find themselves disrespected and disempowered.[4]

As in mothering, the temptation to this kind of dominating behaviour can lead to a dictatorial demand for conformity and obedience or an over-intrusive caring that presumes the other always needs her to do things for him and direct his life. The latter may look like a more servant-based, humble caring but can be, as Hahn suggests, damaging for both the leader and those not allowed to grow up.

Hahn points out that all authority roles are temporary. They may last for differing amounts of time but they are not permanent patterns of relating. She writes: 'We are owned by the Eternal, and all our authority is delegated, derivative, and fragmentary ... authority is not a state of being but an event in time.'[5]

Just as authority roles are temporary, so too are dependencies. This temporary and transitional nature of power and dependency is important to understand. It is true in the formal authority a priest has and also in the many pastoral encounters where people are often dependent on the priest for care.

In her writing about caring, Nel Noddings talks about the 'generous inequality' present in truly caring relationships.[6] This inequality is temporary, shaped by the situation. So someone who is ill may need care during that illness, being dependent on those who look after her. When she is better she will not need to be dependent on such carers. Their care is generous because they do not expect reciprocity of like care. For example, a priest who visits a bereaved family reassures them that for the time of their intense grieving she can be depended on. She will provide practical help through the ritual of the funeral and through sharing wisdom about death and grieving that she has learnt through her work. She will provide emotional and spiritual support appropriate to the individuals who are mourning. She will make herself available but will not expect these people to concern themselves with her needs or her well-being. It is this generous being there for the other without expecting care from them which means that they are able to benefit from the support of a priest. In due course the relationship will change. They will no longer need to depend on the priest to the extent they did in the distressing days of early grief.

In parish ministry some relationships are always experienced as caring, the priest offering pastoral care to people she may not have known before and with whom she may never develop a mutual relationship. This is most likely within larger parishes and more anonymous communities, where people often come for a funeral, wedding or baptism with little continuing relationship with the church. A priest will in her ministry be juggling these encounters alongside other relationships of mutuality, of dependence, independence and interdependence within the congregation and wider community. Many relationships within the community will oscillate as life experiences mean people move in and out of periods of dependency.

For example, a churchwarden and vicar may work together on a project concerning the building. The vicar may happily be dependent on the warden for some of the technical issues since he both knows the building well and in his professional life is trained in aspects of building maintenance. They work in partnership in planning the project and deciding on a strategy for raising the money. In the middle of this process the warden receives worrying news about his elderly mother's health. This raises issues for him about her possible death and all sorts of questions about judgement, heaven and suffering. He now needs the vicar to be his priest and is transitionally dependent on her to offer him the spiritual guidance, prayer and care that he needs to cope at this time. Within their relationship there are complex patterns of dependence and interdependence. There is recognition of where each has areas of expertise and a willingness to trust each to use such expertise for the benefit of the other. Mature adults value and need relationships of dependence as well as independence.

Thus a parish priest will be managing all sorts of relationships where her role means that people depend on her. They expect her to be able to support them spiritually, to show them care and kindness and to provide the rituals of the church, ministering to them in word and sacrament, enabling them to move through the complexities of life. These dependencies are transitional, not permanent, but lasting for the period in which an individual needs support and care. They are for the duration 'generously unequal'. Yet this is not inequality of valuing each person. It goes back to the discussion in the previous chapter about treating people as subjects rather than types.

If we truly recognize the value of the person or people we are caring for then the reciprocity in the relationship comes from seeing them benefit from our responsiveness. The temptation, though, is to prolong this sense of their dependence. For a period we are needed, and although this may be exhausting and draining it feels like being useful; it can feel deeply affirming to be needed. Here we find the danger of relationships that smother rather than encourage growth. This is a serious temptation for both mothers and priests. In a role which has few tangible outcomes clergy can find considerable validation from the times when individuals are most dependent on them. It can feel difficult for clergy to come down after the adrenaline rush of an intense pastoral relationship. The temptation then is to extend that sense of neediness and to keep people dependent. This can look like helpfulness or servant ministry but can all too easily become manipulative and exhausting for all.

We noted earlier that in mothering there is a temptation to over-intrusive care, where a mother is constantly assuming and meeting needs the child has not necessarily expressed. She needs her child to need her and so she keeps him dependent on her in ways that become inappropriate as he grows and develops. This is about a failure to attend to the child and instead to attend to the needs of the mother. She needs to be validated as a 'good' mother by doing what she thinks she should be doing for the child, rather than really understanding her child's actual needs.

A similar temptation is very real in parish ministry, where clergy can for good reasons become over-intrusive in their care for people and communities. This can manifest in different ways: the workaholic who never takes time off because he or she is so needed; the priest who cannot delegate at all because she feels she needs to be in the midst of all situations; the clergy who micromanage perfectly able people because they feel redundant if others can do things for themselves. This intrusive care often arises out of a lack of self-confidence. It may be justified by equating continual self-sacrifice with genuine love. Brita Gill-Austern suggests that when love is seen predominantly as self-sacrifice there is a danger of 'over-functioning on behalf of others'. She writes: 'The less responsibility one takes for one's own life, the more need there is to control others. Although the need to control may masquerade as helpfulness, it is often motivated by a lack of security.'[7]

The temptation to over-intrusive care is exacerbated for mothers and clergy because of the language of love and sacrifice used about both roles. Where loving care is understood to be a continuing process of selfless giving, there is a danger that the focus shifts from what people need to the act of sacrifice itself. The writer Beverly Harrison questions the Christian tendency to value sacrifice for its own sake, reminding us that the ultimate sacrifice of Christ on the cross was a consequence of faithfulness, with the intention of drawing people into relationship with God.[8] The sacrifice was made because it was what was needed for the salvation of those God so loved. Costly suffering may be the consequence of loving service but it should not be valued or sought for its own sake. Our care and concern for others and our witness to the love of God will lead us at times to sacrificial acts, but the reason for such self-giving is in order to engender life and relationship. To be able to give of oneself time and time again means that there has to be a self to give. Mutual, interdependent relationships require two subjects.

Learning to know when to be there and how and when to allow people gradually to move on is an important skill. Being there when people need you but allowing them to find their feet and readjust to life is part of the care. Sometimes the continuing relationship with people will reflect the depth of what has been shared, but in some cases individuals associate the clergy with the deep and painful time and, though grateful for their help, want to distance themselves from someone who was with them at their most vulnerable. Thus clergy are constantly called on to let go, to read the signs and know when to step back and let people move on in their lives.

Collaborative relationships

Parish clergy take on a responsibility of care which means that people will in different ways and at different times be dependent on them. Such dependence is transitional and role-specific. It creates liturgical, pastoral and managerial relationships which are asymmetrical but should never undermine the essential equality of the individuals involved. Times of dependence, it is hoped, will move into times of interdependence and mutuality as individuals and communities mature through the complexities of life events. Within a church community an individual who needed intense support through a difficult redundancy may in time become a key person in the strategy and management of the church buildings. Someone who was drawn into the church community through a painful bereavement may in time become central in the pastoral care of others. A young person benefiting from the teaching and support of the church may mature into a valued youth worker.

The church is to be a living body in which patterns of dependence and interdependence fluctuate so that those in need of care find the support and strength they need and then are often able to give care and support to others. The priest's role is pivotal. A stipendiary priest has the primary focus and time to give to caring for the community and building up the body of Christ in this place. She also has a representational role because of her ordination. This means that although the care and support of all members of the church are outworkings of God's grace, the priest's public association with God and the church means her care explicitly witnesses to God's grace. People receive her ministry as an outworking of the church's ministry and ultimately God's. The authority a parish priest has and the power present in formal and informal relationships are outworkings of her role.

This authority and power needs to be utilized collaboratively. Power does not exist in and of itself, like strength, but arises out of human relationships. Arendt writes that power 'can be divided without decreasing it'[9] and the interplay of power can generate more power. Thus, sharing power does not mean apportioning set amounts, as if it were a cake being cut up, where the more people involved the less there is to go around. Sharing power, like sharing love, can generate more power for all. This is what we mean by empowerment. When interdependence and mutuality are valued, then collaboration, a proper power sharing, becomes a possibility. The complexity is that this power sharing is not neatly controllable. Collaboration, unlike delegation, leaves options open and does not control the outcomes. This involves negotiation and cooperation, moving forward into patterns of relationships and growth that are creative and open-ended. The virtues of humility, trust and forgiveness make true collaboration a possibility.

Humility, in this sense, is a right reading of what is, and is not, appropriately an individual's responsibility: what can and cannot be controlled. Noting that virtues have temptations in two directions means that we can recognize how humility guards against an excessive control, as well as the abnegation of responsibility. The latter fails to offer the suitable care and concern necessary. Hahn connects humility to the interdependent pattern of relationships in the Pauline image of the Church as a body. Humility involves recognizing the gifts you have and those you lack and realizing that others in the community will have different and complementary gifts. She writes: 'But in the Body, leadership and membership have a different relationship. Humility and initiative join hands. If I know I don't "have it all", I will want to bring others' rich potentialities to birth.'[10]

Thus those with the responsibility of leadership need to be discerning in assessing and utilizing the gifts they have and the authority of their role, while always consciously looking at how the gifts of others can build mutually collaborative ways of being together. They need to have a right reading of their own self and find the ways that their gifts can be affirmed and encouraged, while affirming and encouraging the gifts of others. And, in taking the body image seriously, they need to know and rejoice in the reality that it is Jesus who is the head and God on whom all of us are dependent.

To use the gifts of others and to allow power to be shared there needs to be trust. Human interrelationships, and the power they embody, can become fruitful when we can expect others to be trustworthy, to do as they say and to treat us as they have said they will treat us. If people are to rely on their priest to care for them and support them in their vulnerability, she needs to be trustworthy and to act in accordance with the gospel she preaches. Therefore she needs to have integrity and authenticity.

Priests also need to learn to trust others, even when they know that they may do things differently. Delegation means allowing another person to follow your instructions with the idea that they will achieve what you would have done. They implement your vision or the defined blueprint you have chosen. Sometimes this is an appropriate way of working. However, collaboration trusts another to work with you, to find a way for that person to do something which might arrive in a different place and create something which you could not have done or even thought of. Within the church, too often what is called collaborative ministry is simply delegation. Truly collaborative ministry requires a proper trust in others and in the overarching creativity of the Holy Spirit.

Creative collaborative ministry will make mistakes. There will be times when each of us will fail to care properly, will let people down or misunderstand the needs of others, when bright ideas have not been fully thought through or overambitious plans not developed. These are all, to some extent, failures in attention. Arendt calls this 'trespassing': when we hurt others, often unintentionally. Trespassing needs forgiveness. It is interesting that this secular Jew points to Jesus as the one whose teaching on forgiveness is most helpful. She maintains that being able to make and keep promises – that is, to be trustworthy, and to forgive and be forgiven – are necessary for human interaction to build up life-giving communities.

To forgive and be forgiven

In our interrelating, in our community life, we need to be ready to forgive and be forgiven. For a parish priest there will be many times when an apology needs to be made. 'I am sorry, I did not realize that was so important to you', 'I am sorry that I thought this could wait', 'I am sorry that you feel that I have neglected you' and so on. These apologies are not a sign of weakness or, in most cases, of poor ministry. They are often a result of lack of attention to certain people, a slippage into seeing people as types rather than individuals, or of focusing on something else that mattered. They will inevitably happen because clergy are juggling different and often competing demands. So the apology does not necessarily mean that things could have been done differently. It is an acknowledgement of the other's hurt and an opportunity for both to learn through the encounter.

When things become problematic is if there is a pattern of prioritizing demands which always places certain people and needs low down.

When that happens trust is eroded. My mother always felt the need to prioritize her husband, my stepfather, above all other demands, with the end result that none of her children felt able to trust her to be there when they needed her. There were explanations dressed as apologies but no possibility that our needs would ever be great enough to trump even minor ones of his. Trust and forgiveness need to go together. My own children know that over the years I have got things wrong, that they have at times felt unrecognized in a particular need, but the trust that we have means that we can talk these issues through. Sometimes they learn from this about the other priorities in my life and why another's need was at that time greater. At other times I simply need to ask for forgiveness for a failure of attention. Yet I have got it right often enough for them to trust me despite the failings. I am reliable enough.

A parish priest who can genuinely apologize for her failings, who can learn from mistakes and hone her skills of reading people, is not weak but strong in her self-knowledge and care for others. Failures of attention and response can with forgiveness become encounters of growth for all involved. Sometimes, as I left the vicarage to make a visit or attend a difficult meeting, my husband would shout, 'Are you off to fall on your sword again?' This would be because I had realized that the way forward in a particular relationship or discussion required me to be honest about my failings and seek forgiveness, even when these trespasses were entirely unconscious and unforeseen on my part.

On one occasion a sermon in a family service, devised to launch a fundraising appeal, had been worked through with the help of one of the parishioners who helped maintain our gardens. It was about gardening and planting seeds. A throwaway joke about those who helped in the garden being like the team in a popular gardening programme was meant to raise a laugh. Unfortunately, I had failed to think it through and unwittingly hurt one of the other key volunteers who felt, not unfairly, that I was belittling his skills and expertise. It needed a sincere apology from me and time spent understanding a little more of the tensions involved and the hard work offered. I had been focused on the fundraising campaign, trying to work out how to raise the money needed to repoint the tower, improve access to the hall and other building needs. Major issues can take up so much of a priest's attention that she misses the concerns of some of the people she cares for. When this happens she needs to apologize sincerely and seek to repair the damage done to the relationship.

I will address conflict in more detail in Chapter 6. At this point, I am stressing that the power dynamics and the necessary asymmetry in the mutual relationships of a church community mean that failures in relating to people are inevitable. Sometimes we will read things right and other times we will miss some vital clue. If we can be honest with ourselves and others we can accept the failures as means of growing in wisdom and forgive and be forgiven, so that the web of relationships is strengthened. A priest does all of this within the context of the sustaining love of God, the one who is totally trustworthy and mercifully forgiving. He knows our hearts and understands our motivations, and his peace can reassure us when we are over-hard on ourselves and his mercy convict us when we are over-hard on others.

Again, this is why prayer and study are central to the self-understanding of a priest. She has power and authority, but it is transitional and held on trust from God. Others can depend on her because she knows herself to be dependent on God. She can empower others because she continually experiences what it means to be empowered by God. In caring for people and accepting at times that they will be dependent on her, she knows that what look like unequal relationships can still be mutual. The one receiving care, like the child, is not passive but active in the relationship, and out of the giving and receiving of loving attention new things can develop and grow, just as each one of us in our Christian life is not passive in our relationship with God but actively engages in a relationship where we are dependent, deeply profoundly cherished, and yet expected to play a part in the continuing unfolding work of the kingdom of God.

Conclusion

Words like 'dependent', 'power' and 'authority' are difficult for both mothers and clergy because they seem to be at odds with the loving self-giving implicit in the roles. Yet these are powerful roles, even if at times those in them feel powerless and overwhelmed. As Christians we acknowledge that all authority belongs to God and any that we hold is temporary. If we take seriously the idea, explored in

Chapter 3, that all people are gifts, we cherish them as gifts, not posses-
sions, allowing them the luxury of transitional dependency for as long
as that is appropriate. Recognizing that authority and dependency
are transitional means acknowledging that the authority is relation-
ship- and situation-specific. My relationship with my own children
means that I have a level of responsibility which brings authority
with it. We negotiate that authority and dependency over the changing years of their growing up. When other children come to play or
stay they become transitionally my responsibility. As noted in the
first chapter, there is a sense of having a charge to care for these
individuals. Age, experience and the places they are in dictate the
level of care they need. My responsibility is to ask: is it well with these
children now?

A level of scrutiny, of awareness of the situation, and necessary
availability means that I may not need to be hands-on at the moment,
so long as I can respond appropriately when necessary. Growing
children take on more and more activities beyond the maternal
gaze and it can be a costly letting go for a mother to accept this.
There can also be delight and pleasure in the achievements of growing children as they negotiate the world for themselves in different
ways, revealing their unique gifts and strengths. Yet independent
exploration may quickly turn into a dependent cry for help when a
bus is missed, a relationship is fractured or a car is planted on its
side in a ditch! In the next chapter I will look further at this sense
that a priest, like a mother, may be called on at unexpected moments
to resume her role.

In managing these relationships of dependence and interdependence it is important that a priest finds the places and people where
she can be cared for. She too needs at times to receive from others
without needing to give. The Church of England does not have a
particularly good track record of pastoral care for its clergy. Too
often the sense of hierarchy gets in the way of the senior staff's ability
to care, and clergy are left to find supportive care for themselves.
This exacerbates the likelihood of clergy finding their sense of worth
in false patterns of authority, needing to be the boss or the 'needed'
carer, or a combination of both. It takes a secure sense of self to avoid
the temptations of domination or passivity, to be able to give of
oneself without smothering others, to trust in others enough to share
power with them and to know how to forgive and be forgiven.

5

Constantly interruptible

In her book written for new mothers, Naomi Stadlen has a chapter called 'Being instantly interruptible'. This experience of the constant interruptions of her baby's needs is life-changing. In the midst of whatever else she is doing, the child calls her to stop and focus on what he wants. For anyone who had a sense of control over her life before becoming a mother, this disruption is both disorientating and exhausting. She needs to learn a new way of coping with every-day life in relation to these constant interruptions. Lisa Baraitser, in *Maternal Encounters*,[1] suggests that it is about learning a new and different rhythm where the meaning is actually in the interruptions. At one point she likens motherhood to syncopated music where the missed beats, the breaks in the music, are vitally important for the desired rhythm.

I sing in an amateur village choir and I remember our choir director, Rachel, presenting us with a syncopated version of 'Amazing Grace'. We really struggled to get the timing. We thought we knew what we were doing, the tune of 'Amazing Grace' was so familiar, but getting the timing right, adjusting to a new rhythm with unexpected missed beats, nearly defeated us. It took a long time to master, but when we did it was a joy to perform. The breaks, the interruptions, become a new rhythm and for us it became a favourite piece to perform. So in this chapter I will look at the way parish clergy need to learn how to live according to a rhythm full of interruptions. A parish is often referred to as a living, and stipendiary clergy learn what it means to live on the job. They have to weave the interruptions, the breaks, into the linear diary, 'the tune', and integrate them into a meaningful whole. I will suggest that they need to learn how to respond to the interruptions by developing the art of comforting and the virtue of delight.

Living on the job

Parish ministry, like motherhood, involves constant interruptions. When we moved out of the vicarage into our current home, close to the theological college where my husband works, we were at first unnerved by the quiet. The phone was not ringing, the door bell was silent, and the post falling through the letter box was minimal. It was a very different experience living in the vicarage, next to the church hall, with phone calls, visitors and sudden crises meaning we constantly had to reorder our timing and adjust to what needed to be done.

Parish clergy live in the parish, so the boundaries between home and work are inevitably very blurred. For members of the community who are working in regular nine-to-five jobs, church activities need to happen outside their working hours. Their church commitments will be in what might otherwise be leisure time. Thus clergy will inevitably have to work during evenings and weekends. Yet as most congregations contain a mix of ages and circumstances, clergy will also be ministering to those who expect to see them in the daytime. This means that most clergy work a long day, and usually a six-day week often containing days of 10–12 hours of being on duty.

All parish clergy are encouraged to take a full 24 hours off a week, but most experience interruptions at some level, even on days off, especially if they are at home in the vicarage. In a role where an individual has committed to be the priest for these people, how is she meant to respond on a day off when the phone call tells her that a member of the congregation is dying or the church has been broken into? How can she tell the caller at the door that today she is not being the vicar, come back tomorrow?

As well as the interruptions that come with living in the vicarage, clergy face being interrupted when they are out and about. The wearing of a clerical collar identifies them as priests, and in the parish they are usually recognized without the collar. Individuals may use chance meetings with the vicar to raise pastoral issues. Collecting my children from primary school, when I was in parish ministry, might lead to baptism requests, discussions about church issues or requests for a more focused visit. Shopping in the local supermarket, walking the dog or breakfasting in the park café might lead to encounters where I had to focus on what someone was asking or telling me, conscious that my response mattered in how this individual related to the church and possibly to their understanding of God.

Even what had been planned as a relaxing walk with a parishioner could end up being a discussion about theological issues in which I had to remember that as well as a friend I was also the vicar. These interruptions were so often the stuff of meaningful ministry, providing opportunities for welcoming, sharing and educating that could not have been scheduled. The important of such encounters is a reminder that the ministry of a parish priest is not confined to times and places that can easily be delineated as work time and space: the boundaries are blurred.

There are strategies that clergy develop to protect time off and ways in which interruptions can be assessed and prioritized, but there is still something fundamental about the relational nature of being a parish priest that means the interruptions are part of the calling. This availability and commitment to these people is tied up with ideas of service and sacrifice that are deeply embedded in the language and theology around priesthood. Such ideas can be helpful, or deeply damaging, as parish clergy seek to be faithful to God in serving these people in a sacrificially loving way. They need to find ways of being available without totally exhausting themselves.

As with mothering, there is a sense of obligation, faithfulness and reinforced social expectations which maintain that the responsibility to care is not time-limited. Stadlen's insights on the complex transition for professional working women into the role of mothering highlights how countercultural this continuing relationship with its constant interruptions feels. She describes how our education system and many forms of professional work adhere to a 'hurdle system'.[2] We prepare for an event – exams, a particular work project – tackle it and then expect to relax for a while before the next project. In mothering and ordained ministry the responsibility is continuing. A life-changing event has created a mother or a priest, with the demands of that role. There were classes and preparation for both and the birth or ordination service can feel like the hurdle finally jumped, but then the reality of the continuing responsibility for a real person or people has to be faced.

Time works differently

The wider culture values work that can be quantified and contained. Mothering plunges women into a world where time seems to work differently, where what has been neatly planned in a linear way is disrupted by the unpredictable nature of the child's demands. Her priority is to respond to those needs, but she knows that she must do this while retaining her own health and the other relationships and priorities to which she is committed. She comes to realize that the work is never done and that compromises need to be accepted about what is necessary and what is desirable. Alongside the baby's interruptions are continuing tasks and appointments which need to be managed. These linear demands do not disappear but they have to be undertaken while allowing for the interruptions. Compensation in time and rest needs to be found for the ways the child's demands cut across normal patterns of activity and rest.

New mothers are often encouraged to rest when the baby rests, but this can feel difficult if continuing tasks, from tidying the house to keeping up with prior work projects, are also clamouring for attention. A mother may well feel guilty about napping in the afternoon if there are tasks to be done which she cannot do when the baby is awake. She may even feel guilty about the time she spends soothing a restless child or just sitting down enjoying the baby. Stadlen comments that mothers often find it hard to articulate how their time is spent and talk about having got 'nothing done all day' when in fact they have been fully occupied in caring for their baby. The difficulty they have in valuing and articulating this new rhythm of interrupted time means that they often allow others to dismiss it as 'nothing' as well.

For clergy the guilt about working and overworking has similar issues and also more complexities. Like mothers they must somehow manage the constant linear demands which fill their diary with the unexpected demands of pastoral crises. A neatly planned week suddenly gets complicated after the funeral director has rung or a distressed parishioner has called. Yet the planned diary can be hard to adjust. A proper understanding of collaborative ministry means that church committees and meetings are a necessary way of developing shared vision and shared ministry. The planned hours of meetings and visits need to continue alongside the new necessity to meet with the bereaved, to plan a funeral or to sort out a complex situation. As noted in the previous chapter, the adrenalin rush that can come from the interruptions can at times make it hard for clergy to discern what must be done immediately and what can be managed in a more planned way. Like mothers, priests need to develop a wisdom that can discern how urgent a call for help is.

I remember the exhausting experience of a much-loved member of the congregation approaching death through Holy Week one year. My husband was away and the first phone call came through on the Sunday afternoon, which meant finding someone to care for the children as I rushed to the hospital. Over the week I had to decide when and how often I needed to be by his bedside as I managed the demands of a busy Holy Week, with extra services and activities, and the demands of two children on school holidays! Two hours into the Good Friday three-hour devotions I got a message that he was at the last stage. Should I leave others to finish the service and go? The wise priest who was leading the service with me simply told me to stay put: I had done enough, his family were there and I could go after the service to be with him or just with them. Learning how quickly and how intensely to respond is a continuing process, and just like mothering it grows with practice and benefits from the wise advice of others.

Clergy need to learn that others have a claim on their time and care while acknowledging that they cannot meet all the demands made on them. Somehow a balance needs to be found between being appropriately responsive to interruptions and managing a healthy and productive working life. This is where I think clergy can learn from the concept of being 'good enough'. To be good enough is not equivalent to being satisfactory, like the category below 'good' in the original Ofsted reports. Nor is it a resigned 'this will have to be enough because I cannot do more'. Instead, it is about finding a suitable balance in which demands are met well and often enough to provide the security people need to trust the priest and through her see the church and God as trustworthy. Perfection is not possible, nor in the end helpful. The community grows in maturity through relating to a real person with limitations, rather than a super hero, so that they learn to do some things for themselves. Thus clergy, like mothers, need to develop the ability to assess needs quickly. They need to be able to read a situation well and decide whether this interruption requires their full attention now or the need can be deferred or met by someone else.

This is a skill that can be developed and it draws on many of the ideas that I have already talked about. The parish priest needs to be able to attend quickly to the demands made, focusing on what they really are. Thus a call at the door may be anything from an enquiry about the hall to a genuine cry for help. The former, though irritating, can be quickly dealt with and put out of mind. Clearly, the priest is always conscious that her demeanour in dealing with such people may well shape their view of the church, so irritation needs to be kept in check. If such interruptions are frequent it might prompt thoughts about better signage or the production of a leaflet in the vicarage porch with the relevant names and phone numbers for hall bookings. The latter is of course more complex to assess. As with a mother with a distressed child, experience is needed to discern upset from distress and distress from a real crisis. Practice, and proper reflection on practice, enables priests to read body language, to ask appropriate questions and to draw out of people the real issues.

These skills are often underarticulated and sometimes assumed to be inherent rather than learnt. Thus a priest skilled in reading people may simply be assumed to be a naturally good people person. While it is true that some people find it easier to learn these skills than others, to see them as simply personality traits undermines those who have worked hard to develop them and allows others to neglect their development. Reading people well, as we have already noted, requires proper attention, seeing them as they are, not as we expect or fear them to be. It takes embodiment seriously; people speak in body language often more emphatically than in verbalized speech.

These kinds of skills need to be learnt in practice; through watching, listening and responding to people, practical wisdom is developed. We learn through watching how others interact and by analysing the responses we elicit from people. In Chapter 2, I noted the importance of utilizing feelings in this kind of reasoning. Our feelings are a necessary component of how we react to those who make demands on us, and they need to be integrated with our reasoning in order to arrive at a suitable response. These skills of reading people, synthesizing feelings with thinking and finding an appropriate response are rarely articulated by clergy. Yet they are necessary for discerning how to prioritize time and energy. Also, as I have already noted, there is often a trial and error process of discernment as we try to find what is right for this person in this situation. Just as a mother tries various techniques to soothe and quieten a fractious child, so sometimes we have to feel our way into the right response for an individual encounter.

Working to a new rhythm

At the beginning of the chapter I suggested that the constant interruptions mean adjusting to a new rhythm, a syncopated beat. This means accepting that such breaks in rhythm will happen. Priests will be stopped and the pace will be constantly changing. It can become possible to welcome the interruptions, knowing that the meaningful stuff of ministry, the moments we feel that we are mediators of God's grace, can and will happen as unplanned encounters. Clergy may end up feeling most priestly in the unexpected moments when they are truly called on by others.

Baraitser elsewhere in her same book on mothering talks about how a mother negotiates the world differently. She likens a mother with a child in a pushchair to a freerunner practising parkour.[3] Getting around the locality has changed. Things look different from this new perspective. She has to find the correct way around the raised kerbs and endless obstacles which in the past she would hardly notice. Children themselves can also alter the way the world is viewed. Time spent with a young child often slows us down as he pauses, fascinated by the leaves growing in the wall or the buses passing on the road. Looking after my young godson once meant joining his mother on a residential course. She developed her musical skills while I spent lots of time standing by a busy road sharing his excitement each time a lorry went past!

Parish clergy also learn to see the world differently. It may be less important to get from A to B quickly – better to allow time for the chance encounters and the passing conversations. The attitude clergy have to the incidental encounters which 'interrupt' the day makes a difference to how they are perceived. When I was on placement as an ordinand in a lovely Lake District parish, the locals commented unfavourably on the busyness of the vicar. 'He is always walking fast with his head down, no time to stop and chat.' If instead the parish is seen as a place of possible encounters, this changes the way work time is delineated. Knowing that walking in the woods may be time to reflect on one's own or to experience a chance meeting with any number of people allows for a welcoming attitude to either possibility.

An article in *The Tablet* by a parish priest, Nicholas Henshall, described how when his car broke down he began to walk more, becoming in the process a 'three-mile-an-hour vicar'. He describes the kind of encounters he now has as he chooses to walk around his parish changing the way he uses his time: 'If the heart of pastoral ministry is encounter, and if most encounters must take place on other people's turf, then I am content to say that this is the pastoral priority.'[4] His ability to spend time walking might not be possible in all parishes but it is a reminder that slowing down and making space for interruptions, even welcoming them, can enable a rich pastoral ministry. With practice, clergy become good at changing pace, picking up the new rhythms and working with them.

Finding counterpoints

If we understand the interruptions, the encounters that draw us into pastoral ministry, as central to what clergy do and we accept that they could not happen in a planned way, then it follows that the linear pattern, the 'tune' in a sense, needs to adapt to this new rhythm. The insight of Daphne de Marneffe on housework is helpful here. She comments on the way caring for children is often assumed to be an extension of the domestic role of housework. Instead, she suggests we should see housework, the many domestic tasks which help make a house a home, as 'a workable way to be with children'. She goes on to say: 'If my work involves intense intellectual engagement or risky physical labour, tending children simultaneously can only result in frustration, distraction, and incompetence.'[5]

Housework can be interrupted. A child's cry can be met and the hoovering left to be finished later. Housework can also be incorporated into the care of children as they gradually participate, becoming a process for learning about caring for things and places. It can be shared. If the needs of a child become paramount then the ironing can be postponed and someone else may have to fix the supper or hang out the washing. These things will still need to be done, but they can be rearranged, shared and often accomplished while the primary mental energy is engaged with the needs of a child. In fact, at the right time such tasks can be a valued counterpoint to the unending, ever-changing demands of a child. They make little demand on our intellect and can provide satisfying results.

This is of course not to say that housework is the only kind of work that combines easily with childcare, but it does suggest that a counter-point to the constant interruptions can be found in tasks that are less urgent and require less mental and emotional energy. Could this also be an important way of managing the interruptions of parish ministry? I suggest that it can be.

One of the strengths of the role is that, notwithstanding what has been said about demands being made on clergy at unplanned times, parish priests do manage their own timetables. There will be publicly advertised times of services and, as I noted at the beginning, patterns of meetings to ensure a collaborative management of the church's ministry. Interwoven with these are the continuing tasks of pastoral care, administration, managing the buildings, study and broader church, parish and diocesan responsibilities. The priest can, to a certain extent, decide when she does some of these other tasks, and although they need to be done by her, or by others, they often do not have the urgency of the acute demands.

There are many aspects of parish ministry that are not intensely urgent or exhausting. There is pastoral ministry that is continuing and enjoyable as relationships are built up with members of the congregation over time. Visiting such people can often be arranged around the acute interruptions and can provide a gentle calm within the busy diary. A morning or afternoon at the desk can at times be a satisfying counterpoint to engaging with people. Tidiness is not one of my virtues, but when life was overwhelming in the parish I would sometimes ring a friend, who had for a while given me secretarial support, and together we would make piles! That is, she would help me tidy up the desk and study. The sense of satisfaction when order emerged out of the muddle and papers were neatly filed or prepped for action was immense. It had also provided us with time to chat.

Conversations with churchwardens could at times be combined with a walk in the woods or coffee in the café, necessary business done in a relaxed and mutually satisfying way. There were even days when moving all the chairs in church with one colleague, though physically exhausting, could feel like a tangible job well done and an activity shared. And although the services are at planned times they often provide an ordered antidote to the intensity of other forms of min-istry, especially the quiet midweek services. The Wednesday-morning communion demanded little of me except my presence, and the liturgy would carry me as God's grace flowed in me and through me.

Aspects of ministry become important counterpoints to the interruptions. Deep constant currents of relationships with members of the congregation contrast with the intense attention needed to minister to the distressed stranger. The busyness of rushing from one demand to another is halted in the divine services, when we wait on God and let ourselves be carried by the familiar liturgy. The attentive reading of people is counterpoised by the necessary paperwork and the time spent planning, preparing and writing sermons, services, articles and responses to diocesan initiatives. Parish clergy need to understand this rhythm and enable it to work for them.

There will be times when it feels utterly overwhelming but also times of calmer waters where they can catch up with the less demanding activities and find time for the things that recentre them. After the intensity of a difficult bereavement visit, finding some kind of counterpoint can allow a process of re-energizing. Different people will find that different things work: tidying up the desk, visiting an older member of the congregation for a gentle conversation over tea, simply sitting in the church or churchyard absorbing the space or perhaps rejigging the time spent with family so that there is time to see your children at play, or taking the dog out for a good walk. Because clergy do not work a nine-to-five day they should not feel guilty if after some really intense ministry they take some slower time.

Occasionally, I would find in the parish that after some really busy weeks I had a week with less in it – perhaps some cancellations had cleared unexpected space or my busyness meant I had not managed to plan things. Like a young mother who suddenly finds the baby has settled for a long sleep or been taken out by Grandma for a long walk, this should be time to re-energize in whatever way works best. I would calculate how best to use this gift of time. Was I really exhausted and just needing to catch up on some sleep? Or I could use this time to do some of the visiting I really enjoyed, to see individuals from the church who were restful to be with. I could allow some good thinking time, sometimes being in the church and reflecting on how we used the space, thinking ahead to events that would in due course need planning. Or it could be time to read something and actually take in what I was reading! And of course there is always real housework: parish clergy live and work in the same space, and time to keep the house ordered needs to be found. Even if my decision was to have a long nap, read a novel or watch a film, I was aware that this was necessary recharging time. I could not minister well if I did not ensure that I had the energy to meet the demands that would come my way. I could not give of myself if I had no self to give.

That said, of course, one of the difficulties of both ministry and motherhood is that there is always more to be done. And I am aware that in some parish situations the demands are quite overwhelming. Parish priests need to hold on to the reality that the ministry is a corporate one, and find out when and how they need to share the load with others. This may sometimes mean re-educating people's expectations. In many parishes there can be kudos about getting a visit from the vicar, so that the good pastoral care of curates and lay ministers is devalued. I remember having a difficult conversation with a member of the congregation who felt I was neglecting her elderly mother because I had not been visiting, when in fact the curate had been seeing her regularly and keeping me up to date. After we had talked she was able to accept that in this case the pastoral care, and in time the funeral, was carried out by the curate, not because her mother was a less important person but because that had made sense of how we shared out the demands at that time. What helped was that I could allow for the interruption of her concerns, making time to listen while reassuring her that I trusted the ministry of the curate, who was a good caring priest. For me to leap in would not have been right for her family or for the continuing training of the curate. Her interruption was one I needed to listen to but it did not counteract the reality that ministry was shared and that I could trust someone else to meet some of its demands.

In order to prioritize interruptions and to share the workload of ministry with others, clergy need to be honest about where their strengths and weaknesses lie. Self-reflection is a necessary skill, as is the ability to take constructive criticism from others. Mistakes will be made, because we are not always able to be honest about ourselves, and the criticism of others, even when correct, may hit raw nerves. As noted in the previous chapter, this means clergy need to forgive and be forgiven. They need the kinds of reflective conversations that help them to have a realistic sense of being good enough. And they need to work collaboratively, cultivating the kinds of relationships which allow others to take the strain when they are deeply caught up in situations that demand their full attention.

The art of comforting

One of the primary ways a mother learns to respond to her child's interruptions is to comfort him. If it is a cry of distress, need, uncertainty or frustration, ways of soothing and comforting the child are learnt through the practice of caring for him. This begins with a shift of focus and attention on to the child and a mental assessment of the situation while, at the same time, through holding, touching and speaking reassuring words she begins to 'contain' the child's distress. 'It is all right, I am here, what is the problem?' The mother needs to calm herself in order to help calm the child and, in due course, settle him so that he can return to his normal state of playing, exploring or sleeping. Stadlen writes:

> An important part of the mother's comforting depends on her seeing her baby's distress as reasonable. This enables her to treat him with respect. She may not understand why he is crying, but she trusts him. She is not trying to deny his upset, or to get rid of a 'meaningless noise' for her own peace of mind. She feels truly sorry for him and wants to help him.[6]

Comforting is a compassionate response. It feels the reality of another's distress while seeking to calm the situation, assessing what practically can be done, with the aim that the child will be able to move on again, strengthened. This is the root of the word 'comfort' – 'with strength'. The aim is to help another to re-find his or her inner strength and thus his or her ability to cope with the complexities of the world. It is sometimes assumed that this is instinctual but it is in fact learnt through trial and error, through seeing how others comfort and by thinking about how we ourselves have been and would like to be comforted. As the relationship with a child develops, the comforting becomes such an instant response that we do not see the thinking behind it and thus assume it is natural.

A child who has fallen over in a playground is a typical scene that we might observe in any park. As he cries out he is quickly picked up by his mother, who calms him, assesses him for harm and sends him back to play. The mother is interrupted, perhaps from a conversation with someone else or just some idle reflection while her child is occupied. She turns her focus on to the child, rushing over to scoop him up. She acknowledges the distress – 'Oh dear, that was a nasty fall' – while simultaneously making him feel calm and secure. To do this she must calm herself, not allowing her panic to escalate the child's. She makes a quick assessment of any harm, calculating what needs to be done in this situation while continuing to hold and soothe. If the hurt is not too serious she then encourages the child to continue his playing. This is an embodied way of being there for the other, compassionately responding to that person's hurt while assessing his or her need and offering practical and emotional support.

We accept comforting as a part of maternal practice but tend to underestimate its value in adult life, treating comfort as sentimental. Yet it is one of the main ways that clergy deal with the interruptions of pastoral need. The call for help in some form or other interrupts and, like a mother, the priest switches her focus on to the one in need, assessing, soothing and comforting while thinking through what practical help can be given or whether all that she can offer is the comfort of her presence, reassurance and prayer. Many priests have developed their skills as comforters to such an extent that they are barely conscious of the process themselves. By being able to reflect on and name these skills we will be better able both to value them and encourage their development in others.

When interrupted by the news of a difficult bereavement or family tragedy, a parish priest will turn her focus on to the people involved. As she meets them her body language should convey something of her sympathy for them in this situation. The priest will often, like the mother, name what has happened and honour the distress: 'I am so sorry that your mother has just died; it must be so hard for you at the moment.' The words may seem almost platitudinous but they play an important part in comforting the distressed and calming the situation. Through naming the situation and acknowledging that distress, the priest is providing a good response to it and those caught up in it are shown to be reasonable, respected by the priest. This is conveyed both in what is said and also in how it is said. Just as a mother uses the modulation of her voice as part of the calming process, so a priest finds the right tone both to sympathize and show that she is there as a source of strength.

At the same time, the priest is assessing the situation through simple questions, observation and a reading of the other people's body language. 'Was this sudden?' 'Who else in the family is around to support you?' Techniques learnt in previous similar scenarios are tested to see if they are helpful here. Practical advice, if appropriate, is given and arrangements made for continuing action or support. The priest tries to create through her presence a sense of containment of a difficult situation. She is not removing it or offering answers to it – the hurt is genuine and the process of grief will be continuing – but she can comfort from her experience of having seen others pass through this same kind of trauma. As Stadlen says,

> Human comfort is one of the finest strengths that we offer each other. It can be casually given by a touch, a smile, a few words or even by silence. Yet it's very effective. It doesn't usually alter the source of troubles, but it strengthens us so we feel better able to confront them.[7]

Comforting is an art that we begin to learn through the experience of being comforted ourselves. Again, many clergy are already skilled comforters, having been drawn towards the pastoral aspects of ministry through experiences of giving and receiving such care. Yet the art of comforting needs to be continually honed and developed, especially when clergy are consistently called to comfort those they have only just met and who are facing life experiences which they may not have encountered themselves. I have come across good courses for listening well to others but very little that has named or discussed the process of comforting.

We know and value the professional skills of counselling and I would like to see clergy finding the confidence to name comforting as a professional skill which they constantly utilize to strengthen those in distress. In comforting others we draw on our own sense of being strengthened and sustained by the Comforter, the Holy Spirit. A priest is able to walk into the difficult places of people's distress because she knows herself to be 'held' by God. She can offer strength, because she has a perspective beyond the mess and muddle of the here and now: a faith in God's eternal promise of making all things well. This does not mean that she always has answers to people's problems, but it does mean that she can 'hold' them in their troubles, comforting them so that they are strengthened enough to cope with the future. In comforting she needs to guard against the temptation to offer neat answers which deny the reality of people's pain. It is also important that the comforter does not get so distressed that she loses perspective and cannot offer hope.

The discipline and virtue of delight

In the mother–child relationship not all interruptions are cries of distress. There are practical requests for help from children who are momentarily stuck or limited in what they can do. There are also endless interruptions as the child wants the mother to share in his interests and achievements. My almost adult boys can still on occasions burst in to interrupt me with their excitement about a new experience or proud achievement. Ruddick suggests that delight is a virtue mothers need to cultivate. Sometimes it is easy to delight in your child's interests and achievements, but on many other occasions it takes discipline to adjust your focus to appreciate the wonder of something which is far from your own interests.

Thus mothers learn to delight in the various pieces of craftwork carefully carried back from nursery or school. They learn to appreciate the importance of football scores even if they still do not really like or care about football. They try to see the corner of the garden in a new way, adjusting their mind and eyes to understand what the child is delighting in. They learn to appreciate the achievements of their child when he excels in activities and pastimes which they themselves did not encourage. As with all things, practice can improve the capacity to delight and the love and respect that is felt for the child means that, even when a mother does not fully appreciate the achievement, she can recognize and see what it means to the child and delight in that. This affirmation for the child is one of the ways he develops a sense of self-confidence and self-respect.

Parish priests also need to develop the capacity to delight in the joys and achievements of others. The quiet space before a service may be interrupted by the sacristan sharing news of a new grandchild, the slightly nervous first-time flower arranger needing affirmation that what she has produced looks good or the curate needing encouragement for his sermon which will be very different from the one you would have preached. A quiet afternoon in the vicarage may be interrupted by the couple knocking on your door full of joy about their engagement, unaware that they should have waited for the advertised vestry time. Each of these needs to be met with a sense of delight in others' good news and genuine achievements.

Ruddick points out that this virtue and discipline of delight needs to guard against the temptations of self-preoccupation, perfectionism and competitiveness. When we are preoccupied it can be easy to miss the significance of a person's sense of joy or achievement, meaning that we delight too half-heartedly or miss the moment altogether. It can be hard for a priest of a busy church to delight constantly in the joys and achievements of the family members of parishioners, yet stopping to ask the right question about the new grandchild or the son's promotion is a brief gift of time and respect which enhances the relationship and builds up the other person.

Recognizing what others give to the church in time and talents is incredibly important. As one priest says, good ministry involves a constant litany of 'well done' and 'thank you'. It is important that things in church are done well, but when perfectionism means that people are scared that what they can do is not good enough, then their emerging gifts may be stifled and confidence quashed. Sometimes we can be surprised by the way others do things differently from us, making delighting in their achievements easy, but we won't know if they never have the opportunity to try. Priests also have to guard against competitiveness. There will be people who do things better than we can. It can be hard at times to delight when people go on endlessly about how good the Reader's sermons are without that slight fear that we have been outshone.

To delight in the joys and achievements of others is to respect them and encourage them. A secure sense of self and of our own worth helps our delight to be genuine, enabling us truly to rejoice in the blessing of others. Therefore clergy need to discover how their own achievements and joys are affirmed and how others delight in them. As I have already noted, this can be hard for clergy because the rewards many individuals receive for a job well done are not open to them. There are no pay rises, bonuses or award schemes. The chatting mentioned in the previous chapter is an important way mothers affirm each other and can be for clergy if we let it. Affirmation and praise is needed by all of us to help us grow in confidence and flourish.

Clergy need to find spaces and places where they can share the aspects of ministry that have gone well and receive affirmation. Senior clergy need to think about how they can affirm and thank those who day by day are doing good parish ministry. One of the benefits of plenty of delighting is that it seems to be infectious. Those who are genuinely thanked and praised seem to be more ready to thank and praise others. Those whose joys are taken seriously are more interested in the joys of others. Knowing that God delights in us and sees what we do, even if others do not, is deeply important, but sometimes we still need that human affirmation. One year in the quiet days after a busy Christmas my heart sank as I saw the churchwardens walking up the path to the vicarage door. They were interrupting my time of rest and recuperation. 'What now?' I thought as I opened the door. A wonderful bouquet of flowers was handed to me. 'Thank you,' they said, 'for such a wonderful set of Christmas services.'

Multi-attending

Mothers are often portrayed as those who have learnt the art of multi-tasking. They juggle different activities, moving their focus from the meal being cooked to the homework being done, to the shoes that are lost and the complex timing of lifts that needs to be planned for everyone to get to the right activity tomorrow. This is not some mystical female instinct but the learnt response to a multiplicity of responsibilities. They have developed a capacity to switch seamlessly between different things, keeping a watchful eye over a number of activities, ready to act when necessary and appropriate. This involves the capacity to multi-attend. That is, they must take each of these different things seriously, able to focus for as long as necessary on each one while keeping a watching brief over the others.

Parish clergy often find themselves developing these same skills. They may be leading a service while scanning the congregation to see who is there and how they are, making mental notes about pastoral follow-up, worrying about the mother with a young child and whether someone will show her where the quiet toys are and make her feel welcome. They learn how to focus on the conversation after church while also keeping an eye on what is going on around, conscious of who is slipping out and who is hanging around.

Not only do clergy find that they have to switch focus from one activity to another, but on most days they have to move seamlessly

from very different experiences without letting them inappropriately bleed into each other. A tragic bereavement visit to the family
of a young man may be followed by assembly in the infant school
or the mild chaos of the pram service. The news of a parishioner's
marital breakdown shared unexpectedly over a walk is followed by
a committee meeting about the church hall, then a communion
service in a home where most of the congregation have dementia.
The sadness of the bereavement should not eclipse the joy of the
infants singing, the reality of suffering not turn into frustration at
the mundane discussions about keeping the hall toilets clean.

In each space and with each set of people there needs to be
a proper attention to them. Yet the priest cannot fully let go of the
others: there is a funeral to plan, a family to support, a new volunteer
to be found, and she has questions to struggle with about the unfair-
ness of this young death, the complexity of marital commitment and
the pain of its failure and what it is she thinks she is doing in hand-
ing out the body and blood of Christ to people who seem unsure of
who she is and what she is doing. Clergy carry a lot in their heads.
Their days are often full of changing moods; from storms to sunshine,
they move in and out of different encounters, doing their utmost to
be suitably present in each.

Finding the rhythm

Adjusting to the rhythm of parish ministry means accepting the
variety, learning to manage the interruptions and weave the patchwork of encounters together into a meaningful whole. There is a
balance to be found. At times it can be tempting to let the interruptions, in a sense, take over, being continually reactive and finding
a sense of urgency from dashing from one thing to the next. This
may satisfy the craving to be needed and assuage guilt about not
working hard enough. Yet when this happens, aspects of the continuing linear work of ministry can get neglected and a priest can
become exhausted, drained without proper times to recharge, refocus
and top up her own spiritual batteries.

The other temptation is to try to turn the life of a priest into
a more ordered job. This may mean resisting the interruptions by
sending out clear messages that the vicar should only be approached
at certain times and in certain ways, attempting to timetable other

people into the hours that work for you. Again, aspects of good structuring and organization are important. However, this is not a job but a calling to live among and care for these people, so some level of being interruptible is inevitable if people are to develop trust in a priest's ability to care. Many moments of joy, of deep pastoral encounters, of grace and blessing, will be missed if people can only talk by appointment or share the significant, rather than just their everyday cares and delights.

The sense that the vicar is available, and could be called on if needed, can be enough to provide a sense of comfort and well-being for many without their actually having to call, just as a child finds that glancing across to see that his mother is there enables him to pick himself up in the playground and carry on without needing to call out to her. Yet this is only possible when the people know, as the child knows, that if a genuine call for help is made there will be someone to pick them up, comfort them and care for them. The mother, the priest, need to be reliably available, not hovering around like 'helicopter' parents but disposed to come when genuinely needed.

6

Weaning: the art of managing change

There is a familiar joke: 'How many Anglicans does it take to change a light bulb?' 'Five; one to put in the new one and four to admire the old.' It is told to highlight the seeming problems we have in parish ministry coping with change. John Bell, the theologian and hymn writer, once commented that it was not surprising to find resistance to change when we have all grown up singing 'Change and decay in all around I see, O thou who changest not, abide with me.' The association of change with decay, he suggests, is part of the culture which makes implementing change difficult. Yet change is part of any living organization, and if we want growth rather than stagnation, change is necessary. So in this chapter I will look at the issues which arise in parish ministry because change is wanted, resisted and inevitable.

Continuing to use examples from mothering, I will draw on the experiences associated with weaning. I will explore how weaning is understood in mothering, both in its literal sense and then as an example of the constant ways in which mothers need to manage change in their child's life. I will use these ideas to help reflect on the ways change needs to be understood and managed in parish life. Issues of change can often be the starting point for conflict within a church community and so I will discuss some of the ways we can understand and mitigate such conflicts. Much of what I say is common sense but sometimes we need to find ways to state the obvious in order to affirm what is good practice.

Weaning a child

'Weaning' in its specific usage refers to helping young mammals, including humans, move from suckling milk from their mother to eating in both the manner and substance of adult mammals. For babies, the term may be used for weaning them off the breast or more usually for the move from milk to solid food. The verb 'to wean' comes from an old English word meaning to be accustomed to, and originally it was used with a negative prefix: *awenian*. Thus to wean a young child or a young animal from its mother's milk on to solid food was to *un*-accustom the child to feeding from its mother.

Understanding this root helps us to remember that change does not just involve introducing something new but often requires helping people to move away from customs that have been deeply sustaining. To wean people means taking the process of letting go of the familiar as seriously as the process of introducing the new. Change involves losses as well as gains. Such losses may be appropriate; it may be time to give up ways of doing things which no longer serve individuals and communities well. However, to un-accustom people requires sensitivity to what is being lost in order for new things to be appropriated. Mothers learn that for change to be achieved as smoothly as possible much thought, preparation and reflection needs to go into the process.

In the process of weaning, infants are encouraged to change their expectations of how food is delivered. So far they have been used to receiving all that they need through suckling; now it all begins to change. They need to learn new skills: chewing and handling food. They need to experience new tastes and textures and they need to let go of a way of being fed that is all that they have known. This involves a level of trust that this new way of doing things will work and, in time, prove to be a more satisfying process: that what is being given up is worth letting go of for the new. They need to be un-accustomed to one way of doing things and accustomed to another.

This process of weaning a child from milk to solids is just one of the many ways mothers need to manage change in their child's life. Children face many stages where they have to let go of the familiar, being weaned from one way of doing things to another. They move from nappies to managing their own toileting. They move from the Moses basket to the cot and into a bed. They move from playgroup to nursery and on to school. All these changes require negotiation and are often fraught with tensions, successes and failures.

If you spend time in any mother and toddler group you will hear mothers sharing their successes and failures in managing change. The process of potty-training, introducing solids, sleeping in a new bed or cot, will be chatted through as joys and disasters are rehearsed and analysed. Mothers will also be talking about other changes: how to prepare a child for the mother returning to work, for the arrival of a new baby, for the start of nursery or moving to a new house. In fact mothers continually have to think about how to help their child negotiate change, anticipating the concerns of the child and planning ways to make change less stressful and more positive.

As in many areas of mothering, they do not regard themselves as developing skills in change management or conflict resolution; they are just getting on with the job. Yet they know that how they manage change matters. They are often very aware of the problems that can result when change is managed badly. They have experience of seemingly irrational reactions from a child who feels insecure and frightened by specific changes. They may realize how their own complex attitudes to this continual process of change and growth can affect and inhibit their child. A mother who hates mess can find the process of weaning a child on to solid food immensely stressful and the child may then associate eating with the mother's displeasure, uncertain of whether he is the object of it. Mothers also have to deal with external pressures when others, often unasked, pass judgement on how they are or are not managing the process.

In earlier chapters, I described Ruddick's thesis that mothers are always trying to find the balance between three competing demands. We see this tension forcefully in the process of weaning and other change management. How do I help the child to feel secure and safe? How do I help him grow? And how do I deal with the external pressures which dictate that by now he should have reached this stage of independence? Weaning is not an exact science and it needs discernment, imagination and plenty of patience. Through looking at the way these changes are managed, I suggest that we can learn more about how to manage change in parish communities, where helping people to become un-accustomed to familiar ways of doing things is often necessary to allow for growth and development.

Finding a way through all the conflicting advice

The topics of weaning, toilet-training, getting a child to sleep in his own room and other milestones in the early years are constantly debated and open to cultural shifts in what is seen to be good practice. This is not the place to discuss the substance of the debates but it is helpful to note how these affect those engaged in the actual process of caring for a young child. I note that the guidelines given by the NHS in the UK on introducing solids to a baby have changed since I had my first child. These guidelines are presented as expert advice, backed up by the latest scientific and sociological studies. Mothers are encouraged to use the advice of experts on when to introduce change and how to do so. Yet these expert guidelines contend with the advice a mother will receive from past and present practitioners; that is, friends and relatives who have themselves weaned children. Their advice may well conflict with that of the medical authorities and may be conflicting itself, as different practitioners offer different experiences.

There is also a strong social element as a mother will often receive unsolicited advice from all sorts of quarters. This advice can be judgemental and dismissive of a mother's own knowledge or expertise. She also has to contend with the actuality of her own child and her developing capacity to read him. How should she interpret the signs? Is the seeming increase in his desire to feed a sign that her milk is no longer enough for him, as her mother tells her, or, as others suggest, simply a growth spurt that needs her to accept more frequent demands for the breast? Is his refusal to sit on a potty a sign of wilfulness which needs to be curbed or a genuine pointer to his unreadiness to be trained out of nappies at this stage? Subsequent children will be easier to read as successes and failures with the first can be processed as wisdom for the second but, as we have already noted, no two children are the same so mothers will continue to find that weaning and managing other changes is not an exact science.

It follows that, in timing change, mothers need to discern between competing expert advice, some of which knows their specific child and circumstances, some of which does not. Some of the advice makes claims for detailed scientific and statistical evidence and some is based on lived experience of people the mother knows and trusts. The need for change is a given; children do need to progress through these stages. Questions of when and how need discernment and pragmatic wisdom. Yet mothers are also trying to make these decisions alongside other factors in the life of the family, which demand adjustments. Her need or desire to return to work outside the home may dictate the timing of change. A nursery may demand a child be out of nappies even if the mother feels that it is really too early to potty-train him. Factors in her own or the child's health and development may mean change happens earlier or later than desired. Sometimes circumstances force change.

Mothers know all too well that there will be plenty of criticism when they get it wrong and rarely much praise when it is managed well. Because change is inevitable and necessary there tends to be an assumption that when it happens smoothly it is 'natural' and when it is problematic it is either because the mother has failed in some way, probably by taking the wrong advice, or the child is at some level naughty, wilful and not a 'good' baby. I have started by outlining this plethora of advice sought and unsought because it helps to underline the fact that there are rarely clear unequivocal guidelines on how to get change right.

Change in parish settings

Clergy face very similar issues in their role of managing change in parishes. Some kind of change is inevitable because a parish is a living organism made up of people who themselves change and grow, join and leave. Other types of change need to be initiated and managed. For instance, clergy are currently reminded of their responsibility to encourage the growth of the parish. There is an implication that this growth will not happen without intentional management and there is much expert advice offered to clergy about mission and church growth. Some of this advice is backed up with sociological and statistical evidence, some is based on anecdotal evidence from other practitioners, and there are strong feelings about what works and what is best practice. The expert advice is often generic and thus clergy need to translate it into the realities of their particular parish and situation. Alongside this expert advice, often promulgated by the diocese or particular networks of like-minded clergy, is the kind of advice gleaned by fellow practitioners past and present. Some of this advice will inevitably conflict. And clergy also need to contend with parishioners who have lived through previous initiatives which may have offered different recipes for change and growth or left damage from failed expectations. Most vicars have heard the sigh, 'We tried that before and it did not work.'

Increasingly, clergy also have to manage change in parishes which has been forced by circumstances. Falling clergy numbers and stretched diocesan finances lead to the creation of new united benefices, parish

teams and different patterns of ministry. Thus, some clergy are managing quite radical changes in the expectations about stipendiary
ministry or how they collaborate with neighbours. Parishes also have
to contend with changes that come about through unexpected events
such as the serious illness or death of key people, or events in the
wider community that radically alter the pattern of work or well-
being in the area. Many of my colleagues in Sheffield diocese were
in parishes where pit closures had radically altered the community.
Previously there had been relatively prosperous employment, albeit
in a tough trade; now there was large-scale unemployment. The
closure of a major source of employment or the gentrification of
a once run-down area forces change for which the parish church
may, or may not, be ready. What I am suggesting is that parishes, and
the clergy with the charge of caring for them, need to manage change
within a complex mixture of expert advice and external pressures, as
well as the actual relationships with real people in real congregations
who bring their own complex attitudes to change. It can feel overwhelming. It is also often true that criticism of the failures is more
vocal than affirmation of the successes, because successful growth
should and does seem natural.

For both mothers and clergy this array of advice about when and
how change should happen can be utilized constructively. Scientific,
sociological and theological studies can provide insights about actual
and generic practices which may be useful for managing change with
this child, these people. The lived experience of other practitioners
can offer practical wisdom to aid reflection on one's own practice
and suggest different techniques and strategies for moving forward.
In both practices I have used ideas and insights from books and
courses. I was grateful for wise practitioners who at times helped me
think through how I managed changes in my children's lives. I was
also immensely grateful for fellow practitioners who helped me reflect
on the way I handled situations of change in my ministry as a parish
priest, occasionally pointing out aspects that I had failed fully to
understand.

Yet if a mother or a priest is suffering from a lack of self-confidence,
conflicting advice can become paralysing. This can lead to incon-
sistency in the way change is managed, causing unnecessary confusion
for others, or it can sometimes mean sticking rigidly to a definite line
of action, even when evidence shows that this is not really working

for anyone. A mother may be captivated by whatever latest bit of advice she gets, confusing the child who then wants to hold ever closer to the familiar and resist change. Or a mother may become enslaved to a particular expert view on how to wean her child or get him to sleep and persist despite growing tensions on both sides. The child may misread her frustrations – as the neatly followed plan fails to unfold as the book suggests – as frustration and even anger towards him.

Clergy may also be tempted in similar ways. They are not immune to inconsistencies, jumping on each new initiative and confusing those with whom they minister as different ideas about growth, mission and discipleship are implemented without any coherent pattern. They may also be tempted to rely on a particular 'expert' ideology of change and growth even when this is creating levels of tension and unhappiness, perhaps leading to pastoral breakdown. Commitment to this generic pattern may mean that resistance to change is seen as opposition to the leadership or even as opposition to the will of God.

Trial and error and learning from failure

In weaning a child on to a new way of eating, a mother may find that sometimes lovingly cooked food will be refused and even thrown back. Strange likes and dislikes will emerge. A child who appears to be cutting down on his milk consumption will suddenly demand more. A mother will learn to make choices about how and when she introduces new things, accepting that there are times when he, or she, will be tired or distracted and when familiarity is the order of the day. In many of the processes of change in a child's developing independence, mothers know that they are going to use a variety of strategies to see which will work. They also know that what worked today might not work tomorrow; concrete thinking and flexibility are necessary for the process to continue.

Weaning can remind us that the process of change usually requires a certain amount of trial and error. Though suggested methods can help, there is no definitively right way to enable a smooth transition. In weaning a child or making other changes, mothers try out different strategies. New foods are offered – and some are liked! The timing of feeding, the things that help or distract, are noted and evaluated. Ideas are tried out from the expert advice or the suggestions of other practitioners – and some of them work. Trial and error needs to be recognized as a sensible way of introducing and negotiating change that takes seriously the subjectivity of all those involved in the process. If this is accepted then when things do not work, it should be easier to reflect on why, rather than apportion blame.

If we look at this in a parish context we see that trial and error is also a necessary component of introducing change. A parish might decide that a pram service would be a good way of working with younger children and their carers. A day and time is decided on, a structure for the service put together and decisions made about where it will be held and what sort of refreshments might be served. The numbers attending the first few services seem reasonable but they tail off, leaving a small group of regulars. So the project is evaluated. Do we know why those who came at first did not continue? Is the time or day wrong? Are there people who have indicated they would attend if these were changed? Was the content, length, style of the service wrong? Could it be done differently? Was the space wrong, too cold or too uncomfortable? How valuable is it for the small numbers who do come? Should this be relaunched or the ambition for it scaled down? If this is not going to work, then are there different ways to work with those around in the day caring for young children? Such trial and error planning, implementing and evaluating of aspects of ministry are vital if churches are developing and growing. If things go well then it seems to happen seamlessly. If things do not work there needs to be a constructive way of evaluating and rethinking, which does not apportion blame or descend into despair. A growing church needs formal and informal mechanisms to reflect on and evaluate what it is that the church is doing with both new innovations and continuing familiar projects.

Recognizing that trial and error is the right way to manage growth means that parishes should feel able to try out ideas. Subsequent evaluation needs clear-sighted honesty. For such evaluation to happen both clergy and congregations need to feel secure in themselves and their joint commitment to being the Church of God in this place. If a failed project is part of someone's particular vision for the parish, or if the vicar ran a similar event very successfully in her last parish, then it can feel painful to admit that in this place, done this way, at the moment, it is not working. As with the lovingly prepared food the toddler spits out, it can feel like rejection, but it is in fact part of the exploration and learning experiences necessary for growth and maturity. Most of us do not find it easy to handle criticism, so finding ways to acknowledge mistakes and accept that unproductive projects are a normal aspect of building up human communities can help. There are plenty of examples where churches put up with changes which they do not feel are working because they do not want to upset the vicar. Or situations in parishes where clergy are reluctant to make changes they know are necessary because a certain person or people will be deeply hurt by a loss of status. Such situations stifle growth.

A trial and error approach does not mean a lack of planning or preparation. Successful weaning usually involves a lot of thought and preparation. What it does mean is an acceptance that when things do not work it is important not to blame oneself or other people inappropriately. Bruce Reed's work on systemic thinking and parish ministry is extremely helpful in understanding that often problems and conflicts occur because the structures are at fault.[1] We tend to blame people when it may be that things have been organized in a way that confuses or undermines what people are trying to achieve.

In the early years of my ministry in Sheffield I could not understand why decisions we appeared to have made never seemed to translate into action. Was this because I was a poor leader? Was this because some people were deliberately undermining the plans for change? I attended a weekend organized by the Grubb Institute, using Reed's ideas on parish ministry, and started to realize that the problems were structural. The demographics of the congregation meant there was a long period when different key people were on holiday, and the way subcommittees of the PCC had been organized meant that we only really implemented things between September and April; any decisions beyond that seemed to fall into a black hole. Reorganizing how these committees worked, thinking about when the APCM was and how the business of the parish was planned over a year, made an incredible difference. These changes improved things for all of us.

The structures and systems matter immensely, and reflecting on how they are helping or hindering the growth of the parish is vital. Seeming resistance to change may be happening because things have been unwittingly designed to make such change difficult. In Millhouses, this was partly because of a previous incumbent's need to micromanage and another's fear of conflict. If a mother weaning a child is more concerned about keeping him clean than helping him to eat, she may set up a process which makes it hard for him to develop the messy skills of getting food into his mouth. If clergy are more concerned with controlling outcomes or minimizing discussion, they may set up systems that make it hard for new ideas to be implemented. That might not be their intention but it may well be the result.

Understanding what is being given up

In this trial and error way of managing growth, good ideas that one assumes will work may fall flat because the timing is wrong, because some key people are not around to help energize others or because they are not right for this place. They may in fact not be such good ideas. Yet they also may not work because they seem to take away some people's sense of security or tap into bad experiences of loss or change from the past. Problems in managing change arise when insecurity leads people to fear change. In weaning a child mothers learn to accept that progress may not follow a straight line. If we take seriously the sense of un-accustoming, it is understandable that when a child is feeling insecure there is less interest in the new and a desire to rely on the customary way of doing things. When I took my nearly two-year-old on holiday to Portugal, despite being a competent eater at home he rejected most of the strange food and increased his demand for breastfeeding. This was tricky as we were with others who felt that breastfeeding a toddler was wrong. For him there were too many new things at once: it was overwhelming and he wanted the security of the familiar and safe.

An infant who has been provided with most of his food through breastfeeding has of course been dependent on his mother to respond to his demands for food. Yet once the breast has been offered he has in fact had a reasonable control over his feeding. The infant controls how much milk he drinks and the mix between fore and hind milk. He can control the flow, deciding whether to have a quick intense feed or to slow it down. As well as receiving the milk he is experiencing being close to his mother, being held and having to some extent her attention. The shift to solid food initially changes this. His only control over how much he has is by either demanding more or refusing to eat. The physical relationship to the mother is changed from being held against her flesh to a separation face to face, with the child often strapped into a chair. The mother has to be more actively involved in the process. The food has to be made or purchased and the child helped to physically get it into his mouth. The experience is usually messy. It can be anything from great fun for both to a fraught tense situation with tears and tantrums.

A mother needs to think about it from the child's point of view. What does this look like from his perspective? It is important to understand what he is giving up as well as what he is gaining. He is losing some of his autonomy in the feeding process and he is losing a time of being held close. Therefore she might make more time for cuddles to compensate for the lack of physical holding in the new feeding regime. She may need to think about how he can have some level of choice in what he is eating. Weaning is planned. Whether it is a carefully controlled programme or a more relaxed 'child-led' experience, decisions have been made about how this process will happen. Thought goes into how the change is going to be introduced.

In managing all sorts of changes, rituals and transitional objects are used to help move from a secure way of doing things to a new way. A move from a cot to a bed may be helped because Teddy moves too, or because the old cot duvet is allowed to be part of the new bedding. New objects may well be invested with significance: this is your new grown-up drinking cup, your exciting new duvet with Thomas the Tank Engine on it. The new things are both reward and reassurance as they become the new security, the new custom. Stories of past changes are interwoven into the narratives for these changes, in ways that make such changes seem a normal aspect of life. We remind our children of what they were like as we move them on to what they will be. Rituals of mealtimes, bedtimes and other markers of daily life are adapted in ways that blend the familiar with the new.

In this process a mother has to have a kind of double focus. She has an idea of where things should be going but she also has to confront each episode as a unique encounter. If we stick with the experience of eating: she knows that the end aimed at is for her child to be able to feed himself on a variety of foods, eating them in such a way that others can enjoy a meal with him. She knows that this is not going to happen all at once and she needs to work constructively with this child, making decisions about what is important at each stage. There will be days when the focus is on a mixed diet, offering new foods or familiar ones cooked in new ways; these days may not be the best times also to focus on the correct way to get the food into his mouth. It is tempting for all mothers at times simply to stick to what he will eat, to stick to ladling it in neatly rather than letting him smear it round the table, to take control of the situation. Yet although this may be the appropriate response on a day when things are fraught, most mothers know that they will have to return to the experiments of new food and the gradual teaching of table manners if their end goal is to be arrived at.

In managing such changes a mother has constantly to take care that the child does not misread the process. If we think of different kinds of changes in home life we see how important this is. In our culture we put a high emphasis on children sleeping in their own rooms. We see this as beneficial to them and their parents. Yet we know this can be a fraught process because the child who has been used to proximity to the mother can experience this separation as a loss or abandonment. For the child it may appear that this change is about rejection, or simply that without a sense of one of his parents nearby he feels insecure and frightened. How parents experience the child's protests can affect how well the change is managed. If the protests are seen as naughty, irrational and demanding then tensions can escalate.

Recognizing the child's sense of loss and his fears, however irrational, is important. It does not mean that change does not happen; it means that thought needs to go into facilitating it. Helping to articulate the fears and reassure the child is necessary. Taking the fear of monsters under the bed seriously acknowledges that we all have fears about what we cannot control and we need to find constructive ways to alleviate and manage such fears. I know that I am not alone in having spent many nights eating my supper outside my son's bedroom, ready to go in quietly to reassure him that I was still there while firmly maintaining that he was to go to sleep for his own good. Over the years our sons came to trust that if they really called out in need one of us would be there, and so they learnt to sleep.

Valuing the view from the pew

In managing change within a church, thought needs to be given to what is being given up. What this is might not be obvious from the vicar's perspective. My generation of clergy had the experience of introducing new liturgy when *Common Worship* arrived in 2000. It is easy from a theological or aesthetic point of view to welcome some of the changes and to see it as being about words, theological ideas and liturgical movements. However, it was important to realize that for many it involved a process of becoming un-accustomed to words they had learnt off by heart, having to revert to reading the book and adjusting to phrases with different rhythms. I remember how in the earlier introduction of the *ASB* my step-grandmother patiently read the service on to a tape so that my blind grandfather could play and replay the words until he was able to participate comfortably in the service. I wonder if anyone else would have seen that need.

New liturgies, new music and altered choreography can all bring new and fresh insights, re-energizing worship, but they can also make it harder for some to settle into the rhythm of worship. An emphasis on the new and up to date may send out complex messages to those who know that they are old and are perhaps feeling past their sell-by date. In introducing the new there needs to be proper provision for moving at a pace people can manage, for finding appropriate transitional objects and allowing the familiar to be, where possible, intermingled with the new.

When church spaces are rearranged, liturgies differently choreo-graphed and old things replaced with new, it is important for those making changes to try to see what is happening from as many perspectives as possible. Clergy need to know whether some things have been given in memory of someone or some event. It may be that these books are out of date or the cupboard no longer useful, but sensitivity is needed if they speak to some people of deeper things and older relationships. Are there meaningful ways to continue to remember the donors while making a sensible decision to stop using their gifts? This can be a continual issue for parishes where donations are needed to fund change, but what was useful at one stage in the church's life may not be so today. Sensitive handling can help a constructive letting go, but failure to address the issue can lead to misunderstandings and breakdowns in trust.

It is complex in parishes because the same things can have dif-ferent meanings for different people. For example, the statue of St Peter on its niche in the side chapel needs moving to allow for the shelving in the reorganized children's area. It is a rather kitsch statue, out of keeping with many other beautiful artefacts in the church. Should it be relocated, and if so where? Should it simply be moved into the vestry and eventually lost? In the Church of England a faculty (an internal church planning permission) would be required for any such move, but what I am interested in here are the different feelings this may bring up. Some have never really noticed the statue or have dismissed it as a rather unattractive piece; it has no significance and where it goes is of no real concern to them. Others know that it was given by the vicar who was here when they were children and they remember the stories he told about the disciples and the way he inspired and shaped their faith. Some are resentful about the emphasis put on children and feel that the whole 'children's area' is pandering to the failings of modern parents to keep their children under control. Some are worried about whether replacing St Peter with a set of shelves is mildly blasphemous and disrespectful.

This myriad set of feelings around moving one item contains both rational and irrational fears. Such fears need to be heard and acknowledged. Where appropriate they may shape decisions about the change, but even when they do not alter the actuality of this change, ways of respecting and honouring the issues need to be found. How is the past valued and honoured? What are the spiritual and practical implications of the changes being made? Does the church need some more thinking and teaching on how we honour the saints or the place of children in worship? How do we reassure those who are dealing with their own personal journey of ageing, with its constant losses, that they are vitally important members of the church with wisdom and insights to give?

Not all change will be contentious but there always needs to be awareness that things may look very different from the pews, and from different constituencies in the congregation. Those who resist change are not necessarily difficult: they may be witnesses to important aspects of the church's life and history; they may be offering sensible words of caution or expressing the fears others find it hard to articulate. Managing change involves listening to the fears, helping people see what is rational and what irrational, finding rituals and strategies which make transition easier and paying attention to the real issues that may underlie people's sense of insecurity. A weaving together of the familiar and the fresh takes careful consideration. In weaning, transitional objects and rituals of loss and gain often help. Such things can also be useful in helping people to let go and move into new things. It won't always be right for everyone but where possible everyone needs to be helped in the process. This requires patience, imagination and the proper valuing of all the different people God has given to this place.

Narrating change

In managing change, mothers learn how important it is to narrate the process. Words of affirmation and reassurance are given and the benefits of the new ways of doing things regularly presented. Constantly, they make positive statements about growing up, developing new skills and managing new situations. They often use stories to help in the change process – stories from family experience, stories from books and other media. Getting the hang of this new way of doing things, from handling a spoon to coping with nursery school, may feel complicated or scary but a vision is held out of a future where these things will feel normal and will bring many benefits. Change has a purpose, but the process matters. The end does not justify the means because a badly managed process can cause lasting damage. Mothers learn that children can develop phobias and complexes where change has been rushed or poorly managed in other ways. Simply insisting that a child starts to behave like a big boy can lead to a level of insecurity which makes the child regress, longing for the security of the familiar.

In managing change in a parish setting, thought needs to be given to how this change is narrated. What kinds of stories are told to connect these changes to the continuing development of the church's life? What is the vision which shapes this change and how is it communicated? How do the stories of faith from the Bible and tradition help to make sense of this change? Here the preaching and teaching role of clergy is important in giving an overarching vision of this church's ministry and mission. Changing the furniture, books, times of service or aspects of music needs to be explored not for the sake of change but for how this fits into the collective task of worship, witness and service that is appropriate for this church, in this place, at this time. This vision needs to be shared, not imposed, and open for collaborative negotiation.

Within the weaning process, whatever the actual changes being managed, mothers come to learn that their attitudes, their body language, convey as much as the words they use. A child craving attention may well know how to drag out a mealtime when he senses that his mother wants to rush off and do something else. A mother may speak words of encouragement but find the process of feeding or cleaning up a child distasteful, sending mixed messages to a child which he finds hard to interpret. Children are not alone in picking up on the attitudes and body language of those around them. Adults too notice when words and body language seem out of kilter. When managing change in any circumstances, the level of stress and exasperation we feel towards others will be picked up and may well lead to further intransigence or opposition. Adults can also misread such body language; exasperation at the messy processes of change may be misunderstood as lack of interest or even dislike of the people involved.

The end does not justify the means

In Arendt's thinking, which we have explored in earlier chapters, the end does justify the means in terms of a work model that starts with a blueprint and ends with a tangible product. A blueprint is to be followed exactly if the finished product is to match the intention of its designer. Those who help in production do so by delegation, following the plan and not deviating from it. This is a necessary way of working for producing a building that is stable and usable or artefacts that fulfil the purpose for which they were designed. There are some understandings of ministry which maintain that this is also a suitable model for church leadership. The vision for the church is understood as a blueprint designed by those who have understood God's purposes through prayer, study and inspiration. It thus follows that authority needs to be delegated rather than shared, and questioning or seeking to qualify the vision can be characterized as difficult or disobedient behaviour. If, however, we are working towards a collaborative pattern of ministry then the vision is not a fixed blueprint but an unfolding narrative, and the questions, fears, insights and challenges are to be explored as part of the creative process of being the church together. This may mean it takes longer to process change but should mean that people move forward together.

Parish reorganizations are carried out at diocesan level and may leave local people feeling underconsulted. New clergy can find themselves having to manage complex hurts and misunderstandings as they help the people adjust to such changes. There is often a sense of loss, and the story told has been about saving money or managing decline. This can lead to an irreconcilable mental tension in which two conflicting ideas have to be held at once; a constant call to grow alongside a narrative of cutting costs and managing decline. It can feel to the parish as if the decision is imposed from on high with little sense of the perspective from their view.

A friend found herself licensed to care for three parishes. One of these parishes had previously had a vicar living in the large vicarage next to the church. The photocopier and other office equipment had lived in the vicarage and many meetings and practical tasks had been accomplished there. There was no church hall or alternative office. The new vicar lived a drive away, in a different village at the top of the hill. On her arrival the vicarage was sold, the money went into the diocesan purse and the collective parishes found that their expected contribution to the diocesan finance had been increased.

For the people of that parish, loss had followed loss, with a perceived indifference about how they were to manage this new way of ministry. The reorganization was necessary, but the process had not been managed in a way that helped these people adjust to new responsibilities and new ways of doing things. The incoming priest fought a financial battle with the diocese to get enough money to create a practical office/work space in the large church. Time, energy and resources were needed to rebuild trust and help that church to grow.

There are, I know, plenty of good examples where proper processes and careful preparation have led to creative new patterns of working and adjustments to necessary shifts in clergy numbers and parochial autonomy. Yet, sadly, there are still far too many bad examples, where change has been made at times when congregations already feel vulnerable in ways that cause hurt and mistrust and that damage the growth of the church. I noted in the previous chapter the importance of forgiveness in the process of collaboration. Where people have felt trodden on, or their concerns have not been taken seriously, then there is need for genuine apologies to re-establish proper trust.

Sometimes people will have to accept that for the sake of the bigger picture things they would like to hold on to need to be let go of. Strategies and plans for the common good will not always feel good to everyone. It is important, in listening to people's concerns and fears, that special interest groups should not be able to use their sense of hurt to manipulate the process, but they must be acknowledged and their view respectfully considered with an intelligent response that reiterates the vision and the process. Sometimes in managing change a mother does have to say to the child, 'Trust me and go with this.' If a relationship of trust has been established then it is possible for the child to accept that, even if this move looks wrong from his perspective, his mother cares for him and would not deliberately suggest things that could harm him.

Parish priests will find themselves having to narrate policies which affect their congregation that have come from the diocese or wider Church. It is important that the priest has an understanding and trust in the processes and, where appropriate, a voice in developing the vision so that she can find the good news and hold out a positive vision for the life of the community she cares for. It is also important that, just as a mother is prepared at times to do battle with the school, doctor or other specialists on behalf of her child, when necessary the priest might need to fight for the rights of her congregation to be recognized by the wider Church and society. An archdeacon once told me, in the face of some badly managed plans around parish reorganizations, that the end would justify the means. I was all too well aware of the way people felt hurt and marginalized in the process and responded firmly that the end would not justify the means if the process diminished trust, undermined people's knowledge of these places and resulted in damaged relationships.

Conflict

In negotiating between subjects who have their own will and their own ideas about things, conflicts arise. In bringing up children, learning to negotiate and manage conflict is a continuing cause of anxiety. In looking earlier at Ruddick's three demands of mothering we noted that tension, and thus potential conflict, is in a sense built into the practice. In seeking to keep a child safe a mother limits his freedoms, in allowing him to take risks she has to let go of her control and in trying to instil appropriate values, ways of behaving and treating others she has to negotiate the alternative values he will be experiencing beyond her influence. Like most mothers, I have constantly had to counter the accusation that someone else's mother does not think, act or limit freedoms the way that I do! Change is at the heart of conflict. It may be change the mother knows is necessary but the child resists, uncertain of where it is going. Or change a child wants to initiate which a mother resists because she fears where it will lead. Conflict comes when the two independent wills have definite but incompatible views on what is right and how things should proceed. Such views may be reasoned and articulated but often they can feel visceral and hard to put into words.

With children we know that tiredness, too many changes, insecurity, hunger and lack of being able to recognize the other's perspective can all lead to intransigent behaviour and possible conflict. I was amused recently when my son's girlfriend commented on Joe's need for a snack. 'He gets grumpy if he gets hungry,' she said. My mind could instantly go to the countless times we had learnt this fact. A dip in blood sugar was often a prelude to conflict and a timely snack could make life better for us all! This may seem a frivolous example but it is a necessary reminder that conflict is not always about the presenting issues. Conflict can be a manifestation of other factors: stress, unresolved anger or complex family problems can lead to intransigence and people digging their heels in over issues.

The change of use of a set of buildings in the parish raised unexpected local opposition. One man seemed particularly upset, though his objections were not well reasoned. Eventually he came to talk to me and shared a very complex family situation which, through a certain amount of shame, was being kept secret. He realized that the building issue had provided him with what seemed a legitimate space to vent anger and frustration. On reflection he knew that these feelings were about his family, not the buildings. It is not always easy to understand or recognize the underlying factors which lead people to vent their anger or opposition in the wrong places. However, it is always worth considering whether intransigent opposition to a change or course of action may be a pointer to issues that with help could be articulated and shared, even if not easily alleviated.

Sometimes simple things can make a difference. If people are feeling insecure in other aspects of life, finding ways to affirm their usefulness can make it easier for them to cope with change. Thinking about where and when discussions are held can make a difference to how people behave in them. Does this discussion need the formality of tables and chairs or would it be better somewhere more comfortable? If someone is feeling outnumbered, is there a way of making this seem less combative? The college where I work holds its main meeting over afternoon tea; it is hard to get really worked up when eating a delicious chocolate brownie!

Bad behaviour

In both children and adults, some conflict arises because habits of bad behaviour have gone unchecked. Where a child has learnt that throwing a tantrum means he gets what he wanted, he will repeat the exercise. He may even discover that the power simply to threaten such behaviour makes others behave in the way he wants. Like Violet Elizabeth in the *Just William* stories, who could get her way by saying she 'would scream and scream until I am sick', children can learn patterns of behaviour which control those around them. Mothers must learn how and when to tackle such behaviour and name it as wrong. It is not always possible to do this in the midst of conflict; sometimes things need to calm down and then teaching about acceptable behaviour can be reiterated. Consistency and integrity is needed to name what is bad behaviour and resist the temptation to be manipulated by it.

When children are little, mothers have the advantage of being able to enforce behavioural boundaries at times by physically picking a child up or asserting their authority in other ways. Yet for children to learn good behaviour, to develop their conscientiousness, the reasons for not behaving in certain ways must be explained. This often involves helping them to understand the responsibilities we all have for how our behaviour affects other people and other things. Interestingly, this is not about teaching independence, but helping children to understand the complex interdependence of a mature life.

Sadly, there are some adults who have learnt to get their way through bullying or other forms of manipulation. And all of us at times may be tempted to get our own way through an assertion of strength or complex game playing. Thus conflict in parishes can arise out of bad behaviour on the part of adults. Individuals may utilize patterns of behaviour which have worked for them in other places, ignoring the concerns of others. They may use bullying tactics to get their ideas adopted, or narrate their own position as particularly needy or righteous in ways that make others feel bad about suggesting alternative ideas. These kinds of bad behaviour can be found in clergy and parishioners.

In a Scouting group I was involved in, a certain leader would threaten to resign when changes that he disagreed with were proposed. The fear that he would not be easy to replace usually meant that his views won. It was a classic misuse of his power and stifled many creative initiatives of others. Although most people knew that he was manipulating the whole group, no one was prepared to take the risk of calling his bluff and telling him that this was bad behaviour. Where such behaviour has consistently worked for an individual, it is not surprising that he or she continues to use it.

Within the church, as well as bullies we find characters who use other forms of manipulation. When any kind of suffering is unquestionably equated with being Christ-like or humble, those who can claim to be having a hard time can inappropriately silence opposition. People can present their own views or needs as always more important than those of others because of their past experiences, even when these are not directly related to the topic under consideration. Some individuals enjoy playing games with people, drawing some into discussions and excluding others, creating cliques and favourites, so that people agree with them in the hope of getting their attention. I have experienced such behaviour from people inside and outside the church and I recognize the temptation at times to use my power in non-collegiate ways.

Recognizing our own bad behaviour and standing up to it when we encounter it in other people requires a secure sense of self. It also often requires the support and wisdom of others. In naming and stopping bad behaviour in my children, I have needed to work with others so that collectively we present a common stance on what is and is not tolerable. Conversations with the boys' father has at times helped me reflect on where lines need to be drawn, what is an acceptable level of childish naughtiness and what is unacceptable. When dealing with adults we often need the help of wise friends to discern what behaviour can be allowed to pass and when lines need to be firmly drawn. It can be costly to stand up to bad behaviour and usually we need the support of others to sustain us through the process. Yet if bad behaviour is not checked then many individuals may be damaged. Such bad behaviour in the church severely undermines the mission and ministry we are engaged in.

In raising children, managing conflict and developing acceptable behaviour requires consistency from all those involved in their care. At times children try to play adults off against each other, seeing if they can get a better answer somewhere else. When I was first living and working in the vicarage in Sheffield my youngest was cared for at home by Jo, our nanny. He would sometimes wander into my study to ask for something or to tell me that he did not like something Jo had said. I would firmly remind him that she was in charge for the moment and I would back up her position. Occasionally Jo, Martyn and I might need to talk about whether a particular strategy, rule or behaviour was called for, but in our dealings with the children we did our best to ensure that we backed each other up. In parishes, clergy and others involved in leadership positions need to be loyal to each other and back each other up. Where there are differences they need to be discussed between individuals and not allowed to develop into factions. New curates need to be wary of being used by people to undermine the vicar. Training incumbents need to back up curates and to critique or develop their understanding away from others.

Genuine disagreement

There are times when conflict arises because there is a definite difference in what is the right thing to do in a given situation. This involves a more complex process of listening and discussing which arrives at an agreed consensus. The end decision may not be to everyone's liking but the process should mean that everyone feels listened to. In some situations differences will need to be acknowledged and lived with; in others a decision has to be made which will follow one view rather than the other. In practical ways this needs to be modelled as acceptable. In Millhouses we had a debate about how best to use a property which belonged to the church. There were different opinions, ranging from selling it or renting it out to reconfiguring it for regular church activities. This was discussed by the PCC and a decision made by vote. The decision was clearly not the one that I as the vicar had preferred. It was, though, the decision made, and I needed to accept this and work with it.

It is, as we know, far more complex when the disagreements touch on doctrinal or moral issues where compromise is not possible and accepting the majority view unconscionable for some. Here honest, respectful discussions are necessary and there may be ways of holding these differences while staying in community. A theological college staff recently held a frank and open debate in front of their students around the issue of gay marriage. The debate showed that thoughtful, well-read, committed Christians could and did hold different views. Some could talk about how their views had changed, some why they remained the same. These differences could be held in the same community, but this would become problematic in a parish if a policy needed to be agreed upon if and when such marriages were allowed in church. As we know with the continuing debates about women's ministry, holding opposing views in one community can become more and more painful for all. There are no easy answers, but solutions will never happen if genuine disagreements are not properly aired and the fears and concerns they contain are not named and confronted.

Conclusion

In managing change, as with all aspects of ministry, it is necessary to attend to the actuality of the other people involved. What does this change ask of them? What are they being asked to give up and have they a realistic understanding of where the change is taking them? Change needs to be narrated so that people have a sense of both the overarching goal and the process of getting there. Parish clergy have a responsibility for this narration. They need to be clear who or what is driving the change and how it relates to the continuing calling of being the Church in this place. Where there is resistance to change or a tendency to see all novel initiatives as good, there is a responsibility to present the wider picture and help people evaluate what they are doing. Pastoral sensitivity is needed to understand why people are resisting change. Are there underlying issues which need to be addressed? Does this relate to the ways in which change has been mismanaged in the past, in which case how can trust be rebuilt and hurts healed?

Sometimes conflict will arise because people behave badly for different reasons. Bullies need to be resisted and those who manipulate others for their own ends should be challenged. Being nice does not equate to allowing others to trample over you. On occasions parish clergy will need to stand up for their parish and congregation and argue their case with wider authorities. Where differences of opinion persist despite a proper process of listening to different sides of an argument, methods for arriving at a decision need to be agreed. Sometimes ways to hold together different views in the same community can be found. On other occasions a way forward is agreed on and suitable care needs to be given to accustom those opposed to the new reality. Trust, respect and a commitment to the common goal are necessary to keep the community developing and growing through the many changes. Parish ministry involves caring for a changing community. People come in and leave, people age, circumstances in and around the parish change, bringing new challenges and new opportunities. There will be things that need to be let go of, new things to be embraced and a continual process of trying to build up a sense of communal interdependence in this place.

7

The food is in the fridge

A cry can sometimes be heard in my household of 'Mum, the fridge is empty!' This, of course, rarely means an entirely bare fridge but just a lack of the food that the boys like to snack on or use to prepare meals for themselves. As they are on the way to maturity they are good at fending for themselves, so long as I have provided the where-withal. I sometimes say to people that my role as a mother at this stage in their lives is to keep the fridge full and provide lifts when necessary from A to B. There are times, when I have gone to the trouble of lovingly cooking a meal for them, when they are grateful and we enjoy eating and talking together. At other times, though, my effort can seem unappreciated as they tell me they have other plans. My eldest has been far from home this last year and I am pleased to see that he has managed to shop and feed himself in a different country. He has learnt through the years of being fed how to feed himself and also how to feed others.

In previous chapters I have talked about those who are transition-ally dependent on the parish clergy and the time spent in meeting interruptions and caring for those in particular need. In this chapter I want to focus on the many, in a given congregation, who take up little of the priest's time. Clearly, for any of us, however long we have been a Christian, there will be occasions where we need support, but most of the time we need our own version of a full fridge and an occasional lift from A to B. What do I mean by this?

When I was vicar I was aware that there were people in the con-gregation who came regularly to Sunday service and who I knew and appreciated but who took up relatively little of my time. Some of them were involved in other aspects of church life and others were extremely busy in their world of work and so we rarely saw them apart from at one of the Sunday services. These individuals found that there was sufficient in the service they attended to sustain them in their Christian life. There was, in a sense, enough provided for them to be able to feed themselves, and many of them were feeding others beyond the church. Their attendance at church fed and nurtured their faith, enabling them to live authentic Christian lives day by day. The community of the church was the spiritual home where they came to be cared for and sent out from. Parish clergy need to take seriously their role in creating this home, keeping the fridge full and being around, if needed, for the occasional lift!

In this chapter I will look at the role of priest as housekeeper. What does it mean to help to create and maintain a spiritual home where people feel able to feed themselves as well as be fed? I will suggest that this housekeeping role is the area of ministry which can appropriately use the terminology of servant. It is, of course, God who is feeding and nurturing all of us in our faith. Yet the parish priest has an important role in ensuring that the people in her care can access the sustenance from God which they need. She plays a key role in maintaining the spaces, providing the wherewithal for teaching and worship and creating an atmosphere in which the regulars feel at home and the visitors feel welcome. At times the everyday work of maintenance and sustaining a congregation's faith is portrayed as an opposite to the important work of mission and outreach. I will look at this tension and suggest that, rather than being in opposition, the two aspects of ministry are intricately inter-woven and interdependent.

Homemaking and housekeeping

For my children to feel at home, able to help themselves from the fridge and manage many aspects of their own lives, that home has to be maintained and continuously attended to. It also has to have the right kind of ethos. Their at-homeness is a product of the familiar things within the house; they know where to find plates, saucepans, cutlery and the wherewithal to feed themselves. Yet it is also about feeling that this is their space, where they are comfortable and secure. They belong here and can relax.

'Homemaking' is a rather discredited word these days. As women, quite rightly, argued for their right to employment beyond the home, terms like 'homemaking' and 'housewife' have become devalued. The care of the domestic space, housework, is often perceived as non-work because, if done by those who live in the home, it is not paid. Much of homemaking is perceived as a leisure occupation or at least something which needs to be fitted around 'real work'. Yet we do value our homes and are aware that time and effort needs to be put in, not just to keeping them habitable but also in the more ephemeral sense of creating an ethos of homeliness. We recognize this sense of a house feeling like a home even though we find it hard to put into words why that is. In whatever way the balance of work is shared in a particular home, and whatever the resources available, if it feels homely that is because time and effort have been put into caring for the place and those who dwell in it. It is a pity that in encouraging women to seek work outside the home we have unwittingly devalued the words used for creating and maintaining home life. Men and women can and should be involved in this work which, when done well, creates the places in which men, women and children can find security and sustenance.

So before exploring how a parish priest is a kind of homemaker I want to see if we can revalue these domestic terms. It is interesting to think about the word 'housekeeping', which so often implies mundane chores, and to note that it comes from the same root as 'economics' and 'stewardship'. When I was at school we had to study home economics, which mainly meant cooking and sewing but had originally been intended to enable young women to manage the household. There is in all these words an understanding that households need management skills, that to be a steward (from the Anglo-Saxon for house/hall keeper) is to be engaged in economics (from the Greek *oikos*, 'home', and *nemo*, 'to manage'). We tend to think of housekeeping as a feminine role and steward as somehow more masculine.

These words, of course, have roots back to the New Testament and early Church. Jesus in his parables used the image of a steward, *oikonomos*, a household manager, on a number of occasions. The early church was based on the household and the description of the Church as the household of God is used in the New Testament. Households were bigger than our nuclear families, containing a mixture of relatives and workers, employed and enslaved. Until the Christian communities were able to build basilicas in the fourth century, worship happened in domestic spaces. Others have in the past looked at the priest as a steward and the image is retained in the Church of England Ordinal. However, 'steward' is not an everyday image. What happens if we focus less on the steward and more on the familiar, but stereotypically feminine, terminology of a housekeeper or homemaker?

A homemaker is someone responsible for the practical aspects of maintaining a home and its ethos. Ruddick suggests that this requires administrative skills. Home life needs to be planned, organized, budgeted and maintained. She sees the home as 'the headquarters for a mother's organizing and a child's growing'.[1] We often fail to credit mothering and homemaking with this level of organization and management. In the first chapter I critiqued the use of business language for the role of a priest, in terms of target setting and leadership concepts of being in charge. Yet in doing that I do not want to suggest that management skills are unimportant. Instead of drawing on models of management which have been developed for product-based businesses, we need to think of the kinds of management skills necessary for organizing a household.

Michael Sadgrove recently suggested that we can learn something from the ant in Proverbs 6.6; he calls this 'organisational wisdom'.

> What do I mean by organisational wisdom? It certainly includes paying attention to the sound principles of 'economy', *oikonomia*, literally 'household management' about which proverbial wisdom has so much to say. The virtues of time-wisdom (as my colleague Stephen Cherry calls it in one of his books), leading and managing people well, keeping your word, using your resources prudently, planning for the future, responding with agility to crises: all of these are reckoned to be essential in the Hebrew Bible's assessment of practical wisdom if your enterprise is going to flourish.[2]

He comments on the rule of St Benedict which, as well as dealing with the spiritual life of the community, contains many practical sections about organizing the day-to-day aspects of the community's finances and looking after the kitchen utensils and the garden tools. The spiritual life of the community necessitated a good ordering of its practical life: sound management and good stewardship. Church organizations need to value good organizational wisdom, which enables things to be well managed in line with Christian values.

It therefore follows that the life of a parish church requires sound management and good stewardship, because in order to be the place where people come for spiritual sustenance, where God is worshipped, faith developed and the Christian gospel proclaimed, buildings need to be kept clean and in good repair. It requires housekeeping skills. The artefacts used for the services need to be provided, cared for and replenished when necessary. The finances of a parish need to be managed according to good economic principles. Increasingly we use the terminology of stewardship in thinking about the money people give to the running of the church household.

As we noted in the previous chapter, congregations change as people come and go, and as those who stay grow in years and experience. New insights and fashions have to be accommodated without losing the sense of the familiar. Thus the household of the church sometimes needs decluttering and reconfiguring, while always being mindful of what is valuable for people's sense of the familiar and precious. There are everyday tasks which are necessary to keep things running smoothly and larger projects to tackle bigger issues of maintenance or redevelopment. The finances have to be managed to allow for both and, of course, for the unexpected. Poorly maintained buildings which look and feel untidy distract from worship and provide a poor witness to the faith they represent. This is domestic work utilizing the kind of tasks necessary for good homemaking.

The parish priest does not do this alone. There are others within the church community who share legal responsibility for the stewardship of the buildings and finances. There are those who have particular skills and interests to offer in ensuring that all is well managed. It is a collaborative project. It necessitates a lot of meetings. As someone commented to me recently, 'the clue is in the name'. Meetings should be the places where in coming together, literally *meeting*, we are able to collaborate on the ministry in which we share. The priest, with others, shapes the vision and helps to ensure that practical activity is in tune with this vision, creating the ethos of this place. She needs to understand the importance of good stewardship and value all those who help in maintaining and developing this particular parish's buildings and assets.

For many priests this can be a daunting task, as managing finances and maintaining buildings is rarely part of clergy training. She will need the humility necessary to ask advice of others, to rely on the wisdom and knowledge of those she works with in this particular church and in the wider diocese. She will need to show her gratitude for all that others bring to this shared work. It can at times feel frustrating that large amounts of a priest's time are taken up with issues around buildings, distracting her from pastoral work and mission. I will return to this tension at the end of the chapter. The reality is that we have buildings which speak, to those within and beyond, the Christian faith of God. They provide the spaces in which we gather for worship, the spiritual home in which people are fed and learn to mature in faith and from which they are sent out to serve in the world. The art is to help them to feel and function like a well-run home, whatever their shortcomings.

Servants and service

Earlier in this book I referred to Arendt's threefold definitions of human activity. It is interesting to note that domestic housekeeping consists to a great extent in what she terms 'labouring'. Repetitive, cyclical tasks need to be done to keep the show on the road; much of this work is mundane. Arendt reminds us that this kind of work has often been assigned to servants or, in the past, slaves. This of course should not surprise us as a domestic servant is one of the images we often think about when we use the metaphor of being a servant. Such servants were employed to do the mundane, the ordinary everyday tasks of running a household. There was often a hierarchy, with individuals employed as housekeepers and stewards who had considerable responsibility for overseeing other servants, all playing their part in running the household and estate.

If people have the money or the power there are lots of mundane but necessary tasks which they can get someone else to do. Plenty of people pay cleaners, gardeners, secretaries and child minders to do tasks for them so that time is freed to concentrate on other things. We don't like to call them servants but these people provide a service, taking over some of the necessary tasks of life. Without a paid cleaner, members of the household need to do the cleaning or the house becomes dirty, inhospitable and potentially unhealthy. Without a gardener, someone in the household must do some basic gardening or it will revert to weeds. When we talk about clergy being servants, do we understand it in these terms? What are the everyday tasks clergy need to do to free others from having to do them?

Before trying to answer that question it is important to remember that the labouring work of domestic service or church housekeeping can be shared and done collectively. Church cleaning and building maintenance, the purchasing and producing of the necessities for the worshipping life of the church, the moving of chairs and tidying up of hymn books, can and should be shared, but these and other ordinary tasks must be done. In most parishes there will be a mixture of voluntary help and some paid help. Voluntary help creates another aspect of management in organizing rotas and encouraging those who fill them. Paid help brings levels of administration and good budgeting of scarce resources. Paid help also, at times, means that people are caring for the building who might not understand its ethos or purpose.

In many parishes today finding people to take on these necessary tasks is difficult. Households where both parents work, older people with more commitments beyond the parish and dwindling congregations all add to the difficulty of finding volunteers. Church finances and the cost of maintaining buildings mean that there is often little money left to employ people to do these tasks. I suggest these difficulties are exacerbated when we fail to value these roles. It is important to see this church housework as not only necessary but also a worthy way of serving God and our neighbour. As George Herbert put it, drudgery can be divine: 'who sweeps a room as for thy laws, Makes that and the action fine'.

Parish priests may well feel that all of this practical housekeeping work is not what they were trained for. I am not suggesting that this is how they should spend all their time but they should be participating at some level. They should also be honouring and valuing all who take it on. Service work tends to be underappreciated and we need to rediscover the way that the New Testament affirms such service, valuing those servants who give of time and energy to further the work of the church in everyday practical ways. When done well, the domestic work of church life frees up others to come and find their faith renewed and revitalized through the worship and service of the church. Such revitalized faith is necessary for the mission of the church but it needs the underpinning of those who maintain the spaces of worship.

In the home part of the maturing life of my children has been an increasing expectation that they take some part in the tidying up and looking after the home we share. This is partly to share the load but also because they need to have an understanding of the activities which go into making their home habitable and meeting their everyday needs. In time they will have to manage many things for themselves and they should value those who do things for them. In parishes, engaging people in the practical life of the church needs to be seen as a way of offering service to others and to the mission of God in this place.

Parish churches may find that clean-up days which bring the community together can be opportunities for both practical work and deepening fellowship. Finding ways to pair people up for cleaning tasks can provide opportunities for pastoral care and intergenerational friendships. Individuals from the parish who are not regular congregation may well be encouraged to help practically to maintain a building which gives history and stature to the community. In my experience there were days when tidying up the church with a member of the congregation provided a satisfying sense of a job well done, and sweeping up after the flower arrangers was a straightforward task of service to those who were using their skill to enhance our worship.

Worship – spiritual feeding

The domestic tasks of keeping the church buildings comfortable and hospitable constitute, as said above, a shared task which the clergy need to participate in, oversee and celebrate. Yet clean tidy buildings are only valuable for those who use them if they provide the sustenance needed. At the start of this chapter I suggested that putting food in the fridge was one of the ways I provided for the young people, on the way to maturity, who live with me. Parish priests have a primary responsibility for ensuring that the worship, teaching and preaching within the church feeds people adequately so that they can live out authentic Christian lives in the world. William Countryman puts it like this.

> The central business of the ordained is to foster the worship of the church, the sacramental life of religion that reminds us, week by week, to look for the deeper layers of REALITY, to expect God in our midst ... This means that we want clergy to be at home with the sacred institutions, just as we hope, more and more, to find ourselves at home in the presence of the ONE WHO IS.[3]

What kind of servants are priests to be? I would suggest that they are those who ensure that the spiritual food of word and sacrament is adequately provided for those who come to be fed. Countryman reminds us that although the Sunday service is often just an hour or hour and a half once a week, for many in the congregation it is an essential experience which spiritually feeds them for the week ahead. If parish clergy get this right then many will simply come and get what they need without requiring much 'hands-on' care from the priest.

In the domestic setting I try to ensure that there is enough food to eat. Sometimes that food is cooked by me and the children eat it just as I intended, other times they pick and choose or make unlikely concoctions out of what is provided. Sometimes they even add to what is there for all of us, buying things I might not have thought of but find I enjoy once in a while. There are necessary staples and particular favourites. Seasonal variety also shapes what is there and festivals demand a very full fridge with old favourites and special treats. I suggest that this imagery has something to say about what we are doing in crafting the worship and teaching in a parish church. There are necessary staples and occasional treats, seasonal variations and festal feasts, and, because we are catering for a mix of people, there will be things people like and dislike and new tastes that people bring from experiences elsewhere. What matters is that there is the right mixture of wholesome food, familiarity and innovation to allow people to feed well. It needs planning, a willingness at times to be creative and inventive and an awareness of the changing needs of the different members.

In *The Dynamics of Worship* Bruce Reed uses a maternal image to offer an insight into worship. Rather than an image of feeding he draws on the imagery of a young child in a playground who now and then runs back to stand by his mother, sometimes interacting, sometimes just checking she is there, before continuing his play. He describes this as a child 'recharging his courage batteries'.[4] Somehow the reassurance that he is still in the mother's care enables him to play independently from the mother. Reed suggests that through a well-designed act of worship Christians are enabled to recharge their internal sense of being in God's care, thus enabling them to go out into the world secure in their faith. His focus is on eucharistic worship, but the principle can apply to other services. Within the eucharistic liturgy we are reminded of who God is, of our fallen nature and his merciful forgiveness. We find ourselves fed in word and sacrament and then sent out into the world to live and work for God's praise and glory. The role of the clergy is to facilitate this worship but not get in the way of people's experience of God.

Early in my ministry I remember standing at the back of church after the service in conversation with a young teacher in the congregation. She thanked me for my sermon, which she said had been just what she needed to hear. I said I was pleased she had found it helpful as I had been worried it was a little muddled in the middle, to which she replied, 'Oh, I didn't get to the middle.' As time has gone on I know what she meant. There are some sermons I listen to attentively the whole way through, but on other occasions something said will tap into a particular issue I have been thinking and praying about and I might be off on a tangent. This is not a problem if the tangent is the process by which God is speaking to me and I am regrounding my faith.

The liturgy and the music can work in similar ways; sometimes the familiar words are a comfortably ordinary experience and yet, on other occasions, a phrase in a prayer or the words of a hymn or a phrase of music will become extraordinary, taking our hearts and minds into deeper experiences of God or raising for us complex questions of faith. The clergy and those leading worship do not control the experience of those present. Worship is offered and the people, touched by the Holy Spirit, engage in their own way. What they get out of it is, hopefully, a deepening sense of their relationship with God through Christ; how they get there is not something that can be prescribed.

If we return to my opening image, the clergy need not just to ensure that the food is in the fridge but that people can both access it and make use of it. To a great extent children learn how to eat, cook for themselves and care for themselves by the experience of being fed and watching how food is made and prepared. Sometimes they ask for advice. They can get such advice from others in the home more experienced in this process or turn to recipes in books and other media. In order to help themselves and to learn for themselves, they need to feel comfortably at home. They know that they are in a place of security where they belong and where things are provided *for them*. They know that the food will be replenished; there will be enough tomorrow as well as today. They know that they can ask for advice. In our home the food belongs to us all, so it is not like a shared fridge at university where what you can use is restricted.

All this means that the ability of the congregation to take what they need from the service involves far more preparation than the actual content of a given Sunday. Again, it is not something which clergy do alone, but it is a principal part of their ministry to provide, in Sunday services and all other rites of the Church, the spiritual food people need. This is service but of course it is also what Arendt calls action: the building up of communities. These should be places in which people feel at home with God and with their fellow Christians.

People need to feel cherished in order to have that sense of belonging. Ruddick says: 'Home is where children are supposed to return when their world turns heartless, where they centre themselves in the world they are discovering.'[5]

The ethos of a church community needs to be inclusive of its many different members. This draws on issues covered in earlier chapters about how we cherish people and attend well to those present, enabling people to feel that this is their space. As Reed suggests, it is supposed to be the place where people can bring their uncertainties about the world and their questions about faith, finding in the process of worship an experience of being held and nurtured by God: recentring their lives on Christ.

Encouraging people to play their part in the continuing maintenance of the church's life is good but we do need to be mindful of all that they are doing beyond the church. Some might have little time and energy to give to this project because they are giving of themselves elsewhere. Yet we need to ensure that they know their presence as part of a congregation is valuable; they bring something as well as taking what they need for their own life of faith. There needs to be an atmosphere of the church belonging to all its members, not just to a busy clique at the centre. In organizing a parish weekend I was disappointed when, a week before, a family told me they were no longer planning to come. In different ways each of the four of them was important for the balance of the weekend and I would have to rethink how to organize various groups. I sighed as she told me. 'Oh,' I said, 'that is going to make things difficult.' 'It is all right,' she said, 'we will still pay.' I said that I had not even considered the money but was thinking about how much we would miss their presence and how that would change things. She rang me later that day saying they would come.

Churches also need to be welcoming to visitors and newcomers. As with all homes, there will be particular patterns of behaving and inhabiting the space which feel normal to regulars but are unclear to visitors. Therefore it is important that people are attentive to these issues. Where should someone sit? How does a visitor follow the liturgy, join in with singing, understand the choreography of this congregation? Parish clergy need to think through with others in the congregation how to make it easier for people to feel comfortable in the space. Simple things can make a difference. Clear directions in service books or from those leading worship can help new people find their way. Friendly, but not overpowering, steers can be given by those who know their way around. Now and then it helps to talk honestly to visitors about what it feels like to come into the church and negotiate a service. This is particularly important if people are also managing children. We often forget that, these days, there are very few places where people regularly take children and expect them to stay quiet and unoccupied. This is a cultural shift and parents may need help in finding ways of being with young children in church.

When we visit a new country we often need advice about manners: how to greet people, how to eat and ordinary everyday matters. They will be straightforward to those who grew up with them but can feel odd to those unaccustomed to them. This needs to be remembered when people from outside the church visit or join. It needs to be easy and not embarrassing for people to ask, and there needs to be enough self-understanding from those within the community about why they do things this way.

Money

Homemaking and keeping the fridge stocked involves money. The maintenance of a parish church and its regular services requires budgeting to pay the necessary bills. New projects and refurbishments have to be paid for. Like those of many households, parish finances are often precarious, meaning that difficult decisions must be made about which bills take priority. This can be stressful. Parish finance is also difficult for clergy because most of the money needs to come from those they are caring for. I remember discussing my difficulties in organizing a fundraising campaign with Bruce Reed, while on a conference. He told me that I needed a better theology of money. Priests are called on to preach a gospel which is all about free grace and unearned salvation. It can then feel difficult to ask people to pay for the upkeep of the church and its ministry. The New Testament is clear on this: grace is free but the saints are meant to share their money, to give to the needs of others and to support the missionary work of the Church. I needed to learn how to share a vision for the ministry in that place with a realistic account of what it cost, and ask people to give. I found that when I did this the money then came from unexpected places, and to my surprise some people were glad to be asked and happy to give.

Different parishes will be in very different situations in terms of the financial position of the congregation. A good parish priest is aware of the kinds of household budgets these people are managing at home, and it can feel really difficult to ask those on tight budgets to factor in the upkeep of a large church building. Yet the buildings and the work of ministry need financial underpinning. There has to be a vision which situates this need within the current ministry and outreach of this church and the continuing witness to the gospel message. There also has to be realistic presentation of what things cost. Friends who moved to the United States had always considered themselves generous givers to their UK church but found the very different, more open attitude to giving in the USA made them rethink and give far more. As I noted above, there has been a significant cultural change in working patterns so that often churches need to think about paid help where there used to be volunteers. Paying for administrators, youth workers, cleaners and vergers may require a shift in a congregation's understanding about how people's time, energy and money are best used.

Much money, though, is taken up by the buildings. Fundraising to repoint the church tower or replace the boiler is hard work and the whole community has to have a sense that this is necessary for the continuing ministry of the Church in this place. If this is not done and buildings are in poor repair, the space is poorly heated or the access unkempt or ill lit, the life of the parish and its ministry is diminished. This can make life very hard for some parishes struggling to live well in a building which is hard to maintain with little financial support. The legacy of historic buildings, which can often be in the wrong places for today's population, raises difficult issues for the wider Church about when and how certain buildings are no longer fit for purpose. I do not have any easy answers to this or other questions about managing old and expensive buildings, but I am clear that it is not helpful when the maintenance work is portrayed as being in tension with the real missionary work of the church or when the efforts involved are undervalued.

Maintenance and mission

In a proper valuing of the missionary calling of the church there is a temptation to place mission and maintenance in opposition. Maintenance is equated with simply keeping the show on the road, a sort of status quo which lacks vision. When this happens, maintenance is cast as a drag on the real work of the church, a kind of hindrance to the proper work of mission. This is a misunderstanding of both terms. The mission of the Church is resourced and managed from the local church. As we noted above, the faithful need a home in order to be nurtured and cared for so that they might be sent out. This is the root of the word 'mission' – to be sent out. Christians need to be regularly fed so that they might through their lives bear witness to their faith in the wider world. Those exploring the possibilities of faith need a community which can educate and inspire them, sharing their stories of faith and witnessing to the work of God in their lives.

Our faith comes with a long history and the buildings we inhabit speak of those generations of faith. We might find some of these buildings difficult to care for, costly and cumbersome to use. Yet they speak to our wider world. They proclaim a recognizable message of God's presence in the world, a spiritual reality in the midst of where people live and work. In our mission to the world we need to ensure that these buildings witness to a faith that is active, not simply historic. Tidy, cared-for churches with clear signage and reasonable levels of activity witness to the continuation of Christian worship and community service. People do still turn up at church when a life crisis draws them to connect to God or to seek a place of kindness and care.

Maintaining the buildings well, keeping the show on the road and providing the kind of regular worship and teaching that enables Christians to mature in their faith is all important for the mission of the church. A mission action plan could include plans for improving the church heating, making the building a more usable and inviting space. It could include a proper tidy-up of the church grounds and a plan for continuing gardening to create a well-cared-for green space in the heart of a community. It is interesting to note how many of the congregations founded as 'house' churches in the 1980s now have permanent buildings with all the issues around maintenance and finances. They found they needed a space which was a home to both welcome in the faithful and resource their service and mission to the wider community.

Conclusion

Children gain confidence from growing up in a home where they feel cared for, a place in which they belong and where they can return for rest, food and familiarity. My children are at an age where they are often away, sometimes far away, sometimes just at a friend's round the corner. Every now and then they want to be at home 'just to chill'. The security of their home life has enabled them to cope well with new experiences, to explore the world with open hearts and minds. When they come home they want me to fill up the fridge, be around enough to be useful to them but not so much that I invade their space. I feed them, do the washing, provide an enthusiastic listener if they want to recount their adventures and occasionally offer wise advice when asked to reflect on life's complexities. They are mature, independent in many ways and dependent in others. We continue to negotiate and benefit from our interdependence.

Some of the ministry of a parish priest requires hands-on pastoral care of people. Yet not everyone needs this all the time. Clergy need to manage the resources of the parish in such a way that people can do many things for themselves. They need to be homemakers, creating the spaces in which people can come to 'chill' spiritually, where people are fed, cleansed, recharged with faith and reassured of the dependability of the God they worship. They do not do this alone but in partnership with others who take on the servant tasks with them. This involves caring for the day-to-day maintenance of buildings and their contents, overseeing and participating in the domestic tasks of cleaning, tidying, shopping and preparation, managing the finances and planning for the future. It is vitally important that those who take on the servant tasks, voluntarily or paid, are properly credited and thanked for their vital role in the ministry of the church.

In order to manage the resources of the parish well, priests need to have a proper valuing of good organization, planning and budgeting. They will need to work collaboratively with others who have responsibility and concern for these resources. They need to take advice from those who know more about buildings, finance and other areas of expertise. Meetings need to be envisioned as the way collaborative work is achieved, ensuring that all who have a stake in the life of the church can play a part if they so wish. The careful work of sustaining and developing the Church in this place needs a shared vision, just as it needs generous shared giving.

These buildings need to be spiritual homes, places of security and sustenance for the faithful and of hospitality for visitors. Parish priests have a responsibility for creating an ethos of welcome where spiritual food is provided. Through the rituals of worship, in word and sacrament, the wherewithal is offered for people to be sustained in their faith, deepening their relationship with God, strengthening their fellowship with each other and resourcing them to 'go out to love and serve the Lord' in the places where they live and work. Many of these people are mature in their faith and do not need to be spoon fed: they require a rich and varied diet, a skilful blend of the familiar and the unusual. The priest has a responsibility to ensure that what is offered is good quality and to do her best not to get in the way. She is, after all, a servant putting in the work of preparation and presentation so that those who come can feed themselves. In this she is both God's servant, offering the food which he provides, and the congregation's servant as she helps to maintain the spaces and rituals in and through which they can access what God, through the Holy Spirit, will give them.

8

Living up to the calling – being good enough

To be ordained is a privilege. There is an understanding that God has called an individual to this role and blessed that person for it. Within the Church it is recognized as a, if not *the*, vocation. It is, as I have already argued, not simply a profession but an occupation which takes over the entirety of a person's life. It therefore comes with a mass of expectations. As a professional Christian, a priest is assumed to be spiritually mature and confident in her faith. She is expected to behave in authentically Christian ways exhibiting love, care and concern for others, patience, forbearance and a lack of worldly ambition. It is an occupation which seems to have simultaneously a high and low status.

Priests are looked up to but they lack many of the rewards which provide status in other professions. They are simultaneously in charge and in service, with responsibilities for people and communities over whom they have limited sway. For most priests there will be times when it seems hard work, when they do not feel very spiritual, kind or patient, but rather overworked, underpaid and undervalued. Such feelings can be hard to deal with when you have been specially chosen and blessed by God for this work.

Priests are meant to be good and holy, but sometimes idealized models which do not fit the mundane everyday reality of the work can leave individuals feeling inadequate. Theological ideas which stress the grace of ordination can unwittingly imply that good ministry is simply a by-product of ordination, underestimating all the effort which is needed. Here too there are parallels with the experience of mothering. Assumptions about a maternal instinct can imply that mothers are naturally able to love and care for their children and that this takes little active effort. They contend with a dissonance between the way they are idealized, all those saccharine-sweet cards for Mother's Day, and the reality of a lack of status and little acknowledgment for all the hours of hard work. In a practice where love and self-giving are seen as prerequisites, there is often a lack of appreciation for all that is being done. It is simply what mothers are supposed to do, so there is little credit for doing it! Stadlen points out that there are far more ways to talk about what mothers do wrong than there are to affirm what they get right.

> We don't seem to have a problem when it comes to finding fault. We have plenty of words to describe what mothers do when they relate badly to their children ... The trouble is that we seem to have only this kind of negative vocabulary for mothers ... A whole vocabulary is missing to balance all the negative words and phrases.[1]

Feeling guilty

Feelings of maternal guilt are, perhaps, an inevitable outcome of the practice, because of its inbuilt tensions. Mothers cannot keep their children entirely safe, give them everything they need at all times and really love them unconditionally at every moment of the day. Children are brought up in a world the mother cannot control. They have their own wills. As we noted in earlier chapters, perfection in mothering is illusory because the demands of the practice often conflict. Holding the child safe, encouraging his growth and teaching him how to find his place in the social world he inhabits, will inevitably mean juggling priorities. It is a relationship in which two subjects need to negotiate and collaborate. A mother, as Winnicott suggested, can and should only be 'good enough'. So in the role of mothering there is an inbuilt sense of guilt because a mother can never simultaneously meet all of her child's needs.

In earlier chapters I have already noted the different rhythm of a mother's role. The sense of being constantly interrupted, of multi-tasking and juggling different needs can leave her feeling that she never gets things quite right. As de Marneffe says, 'If our self-esteem comes from doing our job well, then the taxing demands and divided attention motherhood introduces can make us feel like we do everything badly.'[2]

Alongside this sense of never quite getting it all right is the guilt that comes from knowing that there are days and moments when a mother gets it wrong. Failures of love and attention are realities for even the most committed mothers.

There are days when we are overtired, quick to criticize and slow to understand, and thus fail to respond well. Days when we wish that our child was a bit more like our neighbour's. Times when we wish he would grow up quicker and times when we want him to need us more, in order to validate all that we have done. And there are of course days when the children themselves behave badly, leading a mother to question whether she has failed in her efforts to bring up reasonable human beings! There are good days when I can take pleasure in the achievements of my mothering and darker days when I can beat myself up for the ways I have failed them. I also know that incredible sense of competitiveness which can creep in when I hear the tales of other children's success and seek to present my own as some kind of trophy.

In drawing parallels between ministry and motherhood we find that this tension of living up to a calling, which is about love and self-giving, is present in both. Just as mothers wrestle with ambivalence and guilt, so do clergy. There are days on which it is hard to feel compassion and care, when certain parishioners arouse annoyance or frustration; times when we wish others would pull their weight and then get frustrated because they have not done it the way we would have done; days when we wish people would just grow up and times when we want them to need us, so that we can justify our own existence.

However hard a parish priest is working, there is always more that could be done, contacts that should have been followed up and initiatives which could have been taken. Even when hard work has been put into a particular project or relationship, people do not always behave as we hoped or expected. There are times for clergy when we wonder if there is any point to this, despairing of these people, the wider Church and even the God who called us. Acknowledging these ambiguous feelings and finding the safe places to reflect on them is important. Often it is because we are tired or feel undervalued or unfairly criticized. As de Marneffe says in the quote above, if our self-esteem comes from doing our job well, it can be hard when we do not know how to quantify that and the demands seem overwhelming. Clergy need to find ways to re-energize and rekindle a sense of God's benediction. Times of retreat, quiet days or even just quiet mornings can often be necessary to refocus on who we are and why we are doing this.

Alongside the ambivalence is guilt: guilt for not being spiritual enough, patient enough and compassionate enough. When the language of ministry implies that love and self-sacrifice are prerequisites of the calling, it can be hard to deal with the times when we do not love, do not even like certain people. It can feel hard to justify a sense of being overworked and underappreciated if sacrificing self is what it is all about. As a priest it is assumed that your prayer life and faith are deep and sustaining, so it is hard when prayer feels perfunctory.

There was a period in my ministry when I was supporting a family whose daughter was extremely ill. Her mother kept telling me that I was an angel, which made me feel guilty. I felt that she saw me as a paragon of the spiritual life and I knew that my prayer life was dry and rushed. I did not feel I was doing very much in the situation and was embarrassed about her gratitude. When I talked this through with my spiritual director she suggested that I should receive this gratitude as God's word to me at this time. Instead of beating myself up about my inadequacies I should accept that God had used me in this place; somehow my presence was a rock in this family's turbulent time. Of course I should continue to work on my prayer life, but in dwelling on my failures I risked undervaluing the work of God, which was happening.

The temptation for clergy to do themselves down is easily as prevalent as the temptation to overinflate their achievements. If we acknowledge that it is God working in the parish, how can we know what would have happened despite us and where our ministry was a means of his grace? If we set unreasonable targets of growth, whose fault is it when they fail: the priest's, the people's or God's?

There are genuine failings which need to be repented of and, where possible, recompensed. The tired grumpiness which leads to sarcastic put-downs in a meeting or dismissive comments to a genuine question need to be admitted and forgiveness sought where appropriate. The individual who feels marginalized must be acknowledged, even if the fault was unintentional and due to real pastoral demands elsewhere. To forgive and be forgiven is central to the building up of genuine relationships of mutuality and trust. The evening office can be a good time to acknowledge our shortcomings before God and seek his forgiveness and grace for amendment of life. Yet there will also be the reality that perfection is not possible because there are inherent tensions in the calling.

As we seek to preserve people's faith while encouraging them to grow and helping them to understand what it is to be acceptable to others and to God, we will need to juggle the priorities. As we seek to help individuals mature in faith while being part of a maturing community, we will need to juggle our time and energy. If we are always available for people they may fail to work out how to care for themselves. There is also the danger that we unwittingly, or knowingly, make people dependent on us and the rituals we provide, rather than on God and his grace. So if failures of attention and missed opportunities are inevitably part of the role of a parish priest, if some neglect is necessary for people to grow, how can we find a constructive way of valuing what we do? This is one of the dilemmas for clergy. It is difficult to know how to measure success.

Misidentifying success and failure

Ruddick suggests that mothers can end up feeling guilty and can assume that they have failed as mothers because they are misidentifying what success looks like.

> I ascribe to mothers not only a humanly ordinary failure to fulfil appropriate ideals but also, and more seriously the articulation of ideals that dangerously misidentify what counts as 'success' or 'failure' in the first place.[3]

This can happen from very young, as people label a child who sleeps through the night as a 'good' child, implying that where that is not happening there is either a bad child or poor parenting. And as children grow up there is a danger that internal hopes and expectations, or external assumptions of success, lead us to equate certain achievements with successful mothering. Thus expectations of what children will be like, how they should behave and what they should achieve are shaped by ideals rather than this child.

A friend tried to fulfil her parents' desire for her to be a doctor. She resat A levels in the desperate hope of getting the grades, but when she did not she began training as a nurse. She loved nursing and was very good at it, but her parents saw this as a failure and found it hard to take any interest in what she was doing. The education they had provided had, in their eyes, failed and they found it hard to see the strength and resilience of a young woman who could reflect on this failure and move into a new constructive future. The competitiveness which creeps in when mothers talk to other mothers, the internal assumptions about where success and happiness are to be found, can lead to a false sense that if your child is not doing as well as others, or not fulfilling your hopes for him, then as a mother you got it wrong. Such misplaced ideas of success can on occasions stifle genuine gifts and achievements. There is a need to return constantly to the question of whether things are well for *this* child, to look for the signs in his life that who he is and what he is doing are right for him.

Ambition in and of itself is not the problem. Where parents offer little sense of what a child can achieve and set the bar way too low, that can be a disincentive to hard work. It is good to have ambitions and hope for the future, but there is a problem when such ambitions are not grounded in reality and particularity. They may then limit the ability to see what is happening and celebrate the successes that do not conform to the ideal. We see this in mothering, but we also see it in the Church.

Currently the Church of England has legitimate concerns about declining numbers and ever tighter financial constraints. Thus there is an emphasis on growth and mission, with initiatives to encourage individual churches to be ambitious about their future. Mission action plans are encouraged, identifying success in terms of increased numbers with a special emphasis on younger people. Clearly, an ambition for evangelism should be part of the church's understanding of the gospel: a desire to share the good news of Jesus Christ to all. Yet we do need to acknowledge that how mission is enacted and how we measure its success are not straightforward. We also need to acknowledge that many clergy find themselves burdened with a call to grow their churches at the same time as being asked to take on more responsibilities, often for more parishes, and to do all of this with fewer stipendiary clergy and less money. Growth may not always look the way we expect it to look. Managing to keep the show on the road, despite fewer resources, may be a success rather than simply managed decline.

In focusing on particular ambitions for growth we need to be careful that we do not overlook the successes which do not fit the projected model. For instance, there is a legitimate concern that children and young people are less and less likely to be involved in a church or to know the stories and songs of the Christian faith. So clergy look at their church congregation with a high number of older people and can end up feeling that they are failing in their task. New members of older years might not be recognized as examples of church growth because they do not fit the profile. I do not want to suggest that we should be complacent about questions of declining numbers of young people, but I do want to maintain that the Church is in danger of undervaluing much of the successful work it is engaged in.

Many ordinary parish churches are doing extremely important and valuable work among older people. On the whole we are good at this and it will be a tragedy if we continue to treat it as an embarrassment. Church communities up and down the country provide supportive nurturing spaces where older people give of their time and energy. Many of these older folk have a depth of prayer life and discipleship which underpins the ministry in a given place. We see examples of people coming to faith in later life, asking deep questions and finding in Christ a hope for their future. As a wider society we face large questions about how we care for older people. With an increasing atomization of family life and breakdowns in community cohesion, local churches offer wisdom and resources about intergenerational communities, caring for the widowed, the lonely and those coping with failing health. In some societies it is seen as perfectly natural that older people are the ones who concentrate on their spiritual life, yet we seem to belittle the many older people in our churches and the incredible wealth of good practice in which the Church is engaged.

In my experience in Millhouses this was an area of church growth. People were drawn into the life of the church through friends, through funeral ministry, through baptism of grandchildren or simply feeling that this was a time in their life to explore questions of life, death and beyond. These individuals were searching for a faith which could sustain them through the changes of life, discovering the joy of Christianity in a refound or entirely new way. The older members of the church were deeply involved in the corporate ministry of the church and this included its mission and outreach, extending friend-ship to those who were lost and lonely, acts of service from lunch clubs to toddlers' groups, as well as practical help in maintaining, developing and financing the church's buildings and activities. Not only are parish churches places in which older people minister and find support and care, they are often places of outreach, taking services into old people's homes and facilitating community groups which support the elderly and housebound. God is at work in this, and churches in which older people are able to minister and be ministered to well are blessings to the wider community which should be celebrated.

In our fears about church decline there is a concern for young people which is justified. However, successful youth work in terms of attracting and maintaining numbers of young people involved in the life of a church is difficult and fickle. The kind of Sunday school and later youth work which was part of the life of an ordinary suburban parish when I was a child and teenager is rare, not because we do not care about this work but because the competition for children's time and attention is immense. Sunday-morning football and other sports leagues for children and young people have taken the place of much of the sporting activity which used to be part of school life. Shopping, leisure activities, TV and other screen-based activities are all options which did not exist on the Sunday mornings of my youth. It is hard for even the most committed parents to make choices for their children about time in Sunday school versus a well-structured and organized Sunday league, especially if they are promising sportsmen. This does not mean that we should give up on children and young people's work but it does mean that we should be realistic about what we count as success. We have to think creatively about how to use resources well and accept the different context in which we are working.

It is important that the Church should find ways to communicate the Christian stories and values to children and young people. The work done in and with schools by teachers, chaplains and visiting clergy and lay workers is vitally important and needs to be affirmed. However, its success should not be measured simply on how many children and young people are in church on a Sunday. It is wonderful when they are, and local churches need to think about how they welcome and retain those who do come, but this is unlikely to be the most successful area of mission in terms of numbers. Managing communities which are intergenerational and enabling children to participate in worship which is not directed at their entertainment is countercultural. It is hard work which takes much creativity and commitment to sustain. It is possible, and we need to find ways to celebrate and learn from where it works. Most often it is about establishing good relationships, developing a sense of belonging across the ages so that old and young invest in each other.

There is much more that could be said about this – too much for this book. At this point I am simply suggesting that clergy and parish churches can often feel inadequate because they have misidentified what success looks like. They are looking back to a supposed golden age in the parish when there was a thriving 1970s youth club or bulging Sunday school, or looking across to the large church up the hill which seems to pull all the young people from the neighbouring parishes, and despairing. Instead they need to be able to look realistically at what this church is doing well, where it needs to develop its expertise and where it needs to support and rejoice in the work of others.

Using the wrong kinds of measurements

Not only is there the danger that we misidentify successes and failures but also the danger that clergy are offered the wrong kinds of measurements for reflecting on their practice. Ways of measuring competency in one organization may not be easily translated into another. For example, during labour my first child caught an infection and needed to spend his first days in hospital. I was given a feeding chart with two columns, one for the time and one for the quantity of milk he had been given. 'How do I fill this in,' I asked the midwife, 'as I am breastfeeding?' She told me to write down the duration of each feed in the column for quantity. I duly did this over the next few days. There were long and short feeds, some long gaps and other times when he seemed to keep feeding. I asked another midwife if she wanted to see the chart. She simply laughed: 'That's only useful for bottle-feeding. You can't tell how much milk a baby has had from how long he has fed. The only way to judge if a breastfed baby is getting enough milk is to look at the baby and see if all is working as it should.'

The chart seemed such a simple way of measuring input and clearly it was useful for those feeding formula milk. It is possible to over- or underfeed a baby on formula, so it is helpful to have a clear record of how much he is getting. Although I was at one level doing the same thing, that is feeding my baby, it was actually a very different process. You cannot overfeed if a baby is only receiving milk directly from the breast. He controls his intake and so long as you are both healthy there should be sufficient for his needs. As the midwife said, this different process needed a different way of being monitored. It required a less exact science and a more nuanced reading of the particular child. There were criteria – was the child having regular wet nappies, did he look bright and engaged, did he feed regularly and comfortably? – but these required judgement and discernment rather than quantifiable amounts, and they would be particular to this child.

When the wrong kind of measurement is applied it is possible to misread the signs of good practice and even at times to undermine it. A friend who had a child in the same hospital also received a chart; she was bottle-feeding this child after a difficult birth and found the chart immensely comforting – she was an accountant! She kept the chart up until her daughter was fully weaned, enjoying her sense of knowing exactly how much milk she was ingesting. She was persuaded to try breastfeeding her next child, a happy healthy boy, but she hated not having the chart. She felt uncertain about what he was getting, unclear about simply trusting that if he looked well he probably was well, and in the end moved quickly on to formula milk and a neatly kept chart of exactly what he was eating. The chart gave her a sense of being in control, affirming her sense of being a good mother. It did no harm but it closed down for her a different way of judging how well she was feeding her child. It narrowed her options, teaching her to rely on the numbers on the chart rather than learning to read her own child.

These charts assumed that only one thing is important in the process of feeding a baby: how much he has consumed. In fact this feeding time is also important on lots of other levels. It is a time in which the child is held. The distance between a child at the breast, or held in the crook of the arm, and a mother's face is the distance which a young baby can focus on. As he feeds he looks and learns this face, as the mother holds and learns this baby; it is a key process in the developing relationship and attachment of child and mother. A breastfeeding mother is also passing on antibodies with her milk; the feeding is stimulating the release of hormones in her body which ensure the production of more milk, encouraging her sense of attachment and, in the earlier days, helping her womb to contract. These hormones prevent ovulation, ensuring that a mother has time to give to this baby.

All of this is unseen but plays a part in the developing relationship of mother and child, promoting attachment. I do acknowledge that it is not always a straightforward process and for some it is a painful and fraught experience, which raises wider questions about how women learn to breastfeed in a culture where the practice is hidden. What I am interested in pointing out is that the emphasis on measurable targets can reduce what is complex and multifaceted into a narrow focus on one element. Even if that element is the most important, much may be lost if we assume that the rest is merely incidental.

The Church of England for good reasons is looking for ways of encouraging good practice and focused ministry. Thus we have seen the introduction of appraisals for experienced clergy, lists of competencies and assessment grids for selection and training of new clergy and mission action plans for all. These have often been lifted from other organizations and tweaked to fit a perceived model of the Church of England. These are tools and, if used responsibly, they can help clergy and parishes reflect on ministerial practice and affirm good ministry. Yet they are often rather blunt tools which reduce complex, multifaceted practice to simple sound bites. There is also a tendency to use both theological and managerial language without any depth of definition, assuming that we all agree on what it means, let alone know how to provide evidence of that understanding.

Many of the assessment tools that the Church is borrowing come from organizations which are clear about their purpose. These tools become more complex and more prone to misidentifying strengths and weaknesses when used in an organization which still finds it difficult to articulate and agree on what its purpose is. As I have tried to argue, it is a complex multifaceted purpose of creating communities where God is worshipped, where people grow up in faith and witness through their lives to the grace of God. Yet this might not look the same or even require the same skill set in all places. Just as good enough mothers can be very different, organizing homes that look and feel different but in which children grow up secure and move towards a balanced maturity, so too it is with good enough priests.

When we begin to talk about the language of 'performance evidence', there is a danger that the focus moves from ministry to meeting targets, from diversity to conformity. There is a danger that in focusing on the specific the incidentals, which are unnamed, may be unvalued and seen as unimportant. In rightly highlighting all the different aspects of ministry, we may end up with a rather functional picture instead of a person in a relationship. Those assessing clergy may become more interested in the completion of a grid than in actually discerning the character of this priest. If parish ministry is essentially a caring relationship, how do we talk meaningfully about the day-to-day work of ministry which must be continuing, sustained and adaptable? How do we value the fact that this priest walks through her parish with a smile on her face and a willingness to stop and chat? That she lives an authentic life among these people who feel comfortable in approaching her for help in their spiritual journey? She may be efficient, but is she able to acknowledge where things went wrong and to be kind when others let her down? She may have done the things she is supposed to have done but how does she make people feel? Our discernment processes need to continue to value this kind of reading.

Growing churches

Growth

In learning to assess whether my breastfed baby was getting enough to eat I had to learn to look at him rather than a chart to see if he was flourishing. That involved his growth. Growth happens where people are healthy and well fed and where all the conditions are right, but it will not look the same numerically for all. With children, the questions around measurable growth are usually raised when it is not happening, when there is failure to thrive. It is accepted that some will be bigger than others, and grow at different rates. However, if a baby is failing to put on any weight or to begin to meet the expected developmental milestones then questions are asked. What might be preventing this: illness, neglect, a lack of certain hormones or nutrients? How can this be helped?

For many mothers one of their roles in life is about helping their child to find self-confidence in his body. Children will often need reassurance that they are OK, attractive and acceptable even though they are not as tall, as blonde, as hunky, as thin or as athletic as others. They often need help to contextualize their reality, understanding that the idealized images are not meant to be an aspiration for all. In adolescents it is not always those who seem to grow fastest who end up as the tallest. Yet if both parents are below average height then hoping to be six feet tall is unrealistic! Children need to be taught healthy habits, to make the best of who they are and what they have. We know that unobtainable body images can lead to despair and self-harm, undermining confidence and blighting lives. At different stages and in different ways children will need affirmation which is realistic, compassionate and delights in the uniqueness of who they are. This is of course even more complex when children have marked differences in their appearance due to disabilities or disfigurement. Here milestones are different and success takes on its own particular places of delight which may be hard for others to recognize.

Churches need healthy growth that is appropriate and the affirmation that their size and shape is acceptable, even if it does not come close to the idealized models offered. If there is no growth, no new people ever join and the congregation is failing to thrive, then important questions need to be asked. Is there some kind of dis-ease in this community? Has there been persistent neglect? What is lacking in terms of resources which could be supplemented? What sort of care does it need to recover? It may even raise the difficult question of whether this is terminal and palliative care is needed to end the ministry in this place well.

In other places it may need to be accepted that growth is there, but slow and steady. This may never be a big church but is it growing into the church it should be, is it healthy and able to play its part in the world? It needs to be acknowledged that differences in situation may mean different kinds of growth and different shapes of healthy church. Contextualized ambitions can be developed when the people and place are properly known. Generic models can offer unobtainable body images which can undermine confidence and stifle the good ministry that is happening. Diocesan and wider church initiatives need to bear this in mind, helping churches find their confidence rather than undermining what is there. We need to delight in the different shapes and sizes.

Mission

Mission is often linked to growth. It is taken to mean anything from direct evangelism to outreach and service to those beyond the church. The way it is often talked about in current terminology implies that it is some kind of separate sphere of ministry, but it is not a separate entity from the rest of parish life. Mission is about looking outwards; it needs to be authentic and collaborative, flowing out of the growing maturity of the Christian community. It is important for parish churches to ensure that they are not becoming cosy clubs and that they understand their responsibility for those beyond the congregation, but this should be a natural outworking of proper teaching about what it means to be the Church.

This collaborative looking out and drawing people in is, by definition, open-ended. It is not possible to control or measure in quantifiable terms the results of the energy and effort expended. Mission fits into Arendt's definition of 'action', which requires different ways of working from the 'work'-based model of blueprints and tangible ends. Therefore planning for mission needs to be open-ended, allowing for the creativity and surprises that come from genuine collaboration as well as the surprises that come from the work of the Holy Spirit. Insights and ideas can come from programmes but they must be contextualized. So whatever else mission action plans are, they must be open to rethinking and rejigging as things unfold. They also need to be embedded in the life of the parish, not some kind of add-on. In my experience the growth in the parish often came in unexpected ways out of the ordinary work of good parish ministry.

Funeral ministry was not done as a form of outreach but as a service to those bereaved, seeking in their time of confusion the comfort of organized religion. It was done well because each person matters to God and this was an act of worship as well as service. Sometimes, through this ministry, people began coming to church. Some were returning to a faith after getting out of the habit. Others were exploring for the first time. They were not always members of the bereaved family. The sad death and funeral of a young child, sensitively handled, brought two different families into the life of the church. They in turn suggested a pram service to which they invited other people. This never grew into a large event but it continued over the years to be a safe space for people to try out the church and teach their children some of the stories and songs of faith.

A wedding well done might lead to the parents of the bride re-engaging with the local church and finding that they wanted to come more often. A baptism service will hopefully bring in that family but might also be the opportunity for other relatives and friends to find their way into the life of the church. After one baptism we gained the child's step-grandfather, who became a regular and valued member of the congregation. The request from a few of the younger mothers in the congregation to re-establish the Mothers' Union became a surprising opportunity for intergenerational friendships and a way to welcome in friends. The hard work of fundraising can itself become an interesting vehicle for mission, with events that draw people in and a focus on why the church matters. These things were done because they were part of the continuing responsibility to care for the people of this parish. The success of such ministry was not measured on how many people then came to church.

If the continuing life of a church is not functioning well, attempts to draw people into the Christian faith will founder. If what is proclaimed and preached is not lived out in the life of the church community, then any attempt at mission is undermined. Thus mission action plans need to focus on the whole life of the church, allowing for growth in unplanned places through the genuine outworking of the community's ministry. Targets may be helpful in certain types of projects but can be deeply demoralizing if inappropriately applied. Thus a target is extremely helpful in a fundraising campaign, or a plan for expanding the readership of the parish magazine or even for improving the church finances. Such targets need to be reasonable, stretching but not overambitious. Campaigns for such projects can have beginnings and ends with proper evaluation.

Projects about growth, about welcoming new members into the church or deepening the discipleship of those already there, are not suitable for target-based assessments. That does not mean that there are no ambitions for these, no programmes which might be developed to encourage such growth. What it does mean is that this growth is not easy to measure according to neat numerical scales. The speed and depth of growth is not easily quantifiable and some work may only bear fruit years down the line.

A healthy church is one which is ready to welcome new people and which cares well for all those who come regularly. It is a spiritual home in which people feel well fed, well cared for and more than happy to invite others in. It will probably not look like the church down the road or quite match the church in the book, but it will have a good sense of what it can and should be. Some clergy will be tasked with caring for churches in difficult places, where simply staying alive is a massive achievement. Some congregations will need plenty of affirmation to help them find self-confidence, because they do not look like the 'successful' places. Some churches may in the end teach us all to think differently about what is healthy, what is successful and how we understand the grace and mission of God at work in the world.

Fusing being and doing

Stadlen suggests that we do not have enough vocabulary to talk about the things mothers do, all that ensures their children grow up into reasonably balanced, healthy adults. There is a similar problem in the Church. How do we find the kind of language which affirms ordinary, good enough parish ministry that helps churches to be healthy and growing well – churches in which clergy lovingly care for the less obviously beautiful people and places? There is not a simple phrase to describe a priest who is good at building up relationships of trust, which make people feel comfortable and secure, knowing they could turn to her if they were in distress but not making them feel beholden to her. Therefore it is harder to put this on a check list, though all of us want to attend a church with a priest like this.

The funeral directors usually know the priests who are good at taking funerals, but how do we describe this? It involves listening well to the bereaved, being sensitive and flexible, and putting together a service which speaks knowingly of the deceased and provides hope, all within the allotted 25 minutes! It won't be the same formula for all; a number of different priests might be really good at taking funerals but actually do them quite differently. It is about attitudes, ways of thinking and behaving which mean that what is done suitably meets the needs of those for whom it is done.

This involves a proper fusion of being and doing. Too often they are discussed as if they are opposites pulling in different directions.

This is partly due to a tendency to equate being with quiet contemplation, mapping arguments about contemplative and active religious life inappropriately on to what is an active life. To be engaged in parish ministry is to have taken on an active role in the church. There is plenty to do. Yet the character of the one who does it makes the difference to how it is received. The being matters. We know this in so many areas of life. A doctor or nurse can do the same medical procedures but with different attitudes. When these are done with a genuine concern for the patient, treating him or her as an important individual, thinking about it from the patient's point of view, then the patient feels cared for. When they are done efficiently but without interest, the patient can feel undervalued and uncared for.

There has been much discussion recently about how a target-driven culture in the health service has lost the vital elements that meant people felt cared for. At its worst this has led to places where targets may be met but people are seriously neglected. There is so much more to care than the specific tasks. Being a care-full person requires an attitude of attention towards others. It requires the kind of virtues this book has highlighted: humility, realism, compassion, delight and trust. These virtues and attitudes do not happen without practice and a conscious reflection on practice.

For parish priests a care-full character needs to be developed through practice and the honing of such practice. Reflection on practice should happen through private reflection, in conversation with others and in prayerful attending to God. This is active, though of course a different kind of activity from the busyness of doing all that the role demands. For most of us the doing and the reflecting on doing are interwoven. They become part of the trial and error process of learning how to respond appropriately to these people as a witness to the gracious love of God. This is about being attentive.

In being with someone we are seeking the right words to say, the right decisions to make and the appropriate things to do, praying for God's guidance as we make those judgements. Away from a situation we reflect on it, we may discuss it with others – 'Was that the right thing to do in that situation?' – and we bring it before God in prayer, asking that what we did may be used by him for the good of the other and the furthering of the kingdom. In this process thinking and feeling, action and reflection, being and doing are all utilized in a synthesized practice of doing one's best. It is an art, not a science.

There are no formulas which would result in getting it right every time. The aim is to develop the kind of practical wisdom which means that it is right enough, often enough. This needs to be combined with the humility which can admit where it is not right, seeking forgiveness and the insight necessary to put things right.

In reflecting on good practice there needs to be a richer language to talk about what it is that is good. I have tried in this book to offer some language and imagery to help, but it will not work for everyone. I hope, though, that it will encourage more thinking and a move away from the rather empty language of leadership into richer metaphorical language which connects to what people do. In earlier chapters I talked about the art of comforting, of cherishing and delighting in people. It would be good to feel that a parish priest could talk about the way she has developed and used her ability to comfort, that this might get into an appraisal or assessment. It is possible to discuss, and train people in, the art of comforting. It is a different skill from counselling but, just as people are now more aware that listening skills are valuable, perhaps clergy could begin to own their comforting skills. I have also suggested that cherishing is an art and a skill. Again, I would love this to be the kind of terminology discussed in terms of good practice. It would be interesting to reflect on whether the bishop, the archdeacon or the vicar is good at cherishing people. Has each one developed the discipline of attending well and delighting in the joys and achievements of others?

I hope that in this book I have opened up some different ways of looking at and talking about what clergy are doing. It is not always easy; it can feel at times mundane and ordinary with plenty to do and little reward for doing it. The joys, though, as in mothering, are often unsolicited: the simple moments when others flourish and you know that your care has played a part. The incredible satisfaction when your children behave as you have taught them to behave, unthinkingly and graciously, has its parallels in ministry. Those moments when people show the maturity of faith they have developed, when the care and ministry of the church functions well without the need for the priest's hands-on direction, when things you have lovingly prepared are appreciated and when incidental gifts flourish, blessing many. Celebrating such moments, the joys and successes, is a necessary antidote to the days when it feels as though nothing has actually been done.

For those clergy, in senior positions, who have pastoral care of priests, it should be a priority to find ways of affirming and celebrating good honest parish ministry. Initiatives for growth and mission need to be delivered in ways that encourage contextualization. Such initiatives need to have affirmation built in and encourage genuine collaboration which might reshape and reprioritize any outcomes. Appraisals need to be genuinely about attending to the priest within the relationship of their role, understanding context and looking for signs of healthy relationships of growing interdependence. The ordinary everyday work needs to be better named and better appreciated.

A good enough church

I had the benefit of growing up in an ordinary good parish church. It was a rather unattractive redbrick building from the end of the nineteenth century. It served a part of suburbia on the edge of London which had seen better days. It was definitely not a destination church. It was a church that was a community, where a young girl in an unconventional family found a welcome. I learnt through the Sunday school, the youth work and the Sunday services about the Christian faith, but perhaps most importantly I felt at home and I felt cared for. I cannot remember the content of many sermons, though there are a few that have stayed with me. I remember hymns and songs sung and the people I sang them with. There were times in my teenage years when I thought it was a bit boring, too safe, too staid. I visited other places looking for excitement but I always knew I would be welcome at home.

It was a mixed community, intergenerational and diverse. It welcomed in some unusual characters and seemed to find ways of affirming them. Perhaps the vicar's experience leading a church in Africa had helped him see the importance of making community; perhaps the maturity of many older people helped to create the safe space for those of us working out how to grow up. It was a family church in which being an unconventional family did not seem to matter. Through complex and difficult teenage years it held me safe and helped me grow. As I look back I could try and analyse the various things that worked well but in doing so I might fail to describe what really mattered. What I remember best is the essence of the place and the encouragement it gave me to do my best to love God and my neighbour, learning to recognize the rich variety of those neighbours near and far.

It was not perfect. Even from my younger outlook I could see that there were times of tension, that not everyone agreed about what the priorities were and how to move towards them. There were normal issues about finances, building developments, choice of music, how to integrate the young and reach out to the wider parish. I remember things that worked and things that did not work so well. I remember taking risks and trying out ideas. It was a church that for many was 'good enough'. I was not the only person who found there a faith to sustain me through the complexities of life, a faith that I could take out into the world and share with others, a calling to serve and a willingness to try my best to respond to the call. So this book pays tribute to the clergy and people of that parish and to the many clergy working collaboratively in parishes in all sorts of different circumstances doing good enough ministry, creating and sustaining spiritual homes in which people can grow up into Christ, from which they can go out into the world bearing witness to Christ, and to which they can return for sustenance and care, renewing their dependency on the love of God made manifest in Christ Jesus.

Conclusion: integrating the whole

Parish ministry, like mothering, is a way of life. Its rhythms do not conform to traditional boundaries between work and home, on and off duty, public and private space. That does not mean that there is no time off, no private spaces and no proper home life, just that boundaries are blurred and the times of work and rest are not so easily predicted. Those who move into these practices learn to move to a different beat, to know that the interruptions are as central to the meaning as the organized and planned elements. They need to develop an attentiveness which enables them to respond quickly to a change in pace, the urgency of a cry for help or the slowing down to delight in the wonder of ordinary miracles. Clergy learn to weave the ordered organizing necessary to provide the places that sustain people with the openness to chance surprise and unplanned encounters. Like a patchwork quilt, their days contain different colours and textures which need to be held together in a creative whole.

In suggesting that parish ministry is like mothering I am offering an image that integrates these different experiences. Mothers are organizers, carers, comforters and admonishers, providers of food, teachers, playmates, sounding boards, sympathizers, storytellers and boundary setters. As we noted from Ruddick's work, they are engaged in a practice with inherent tensions. They are holding their children safe while encouraging them to take risks and grow up. They are doing both of these while trying to teach their children the values and ways of behaving which will enable them to be acceptable, fit to live well with others. Thus mothers are continual moving between actions which respond to these demands, thinking on the hoof about what is best for this child, at this time, in this place. There are no formulas to provide the right answers: they need to develop the wisdom of practice and cultivate virtues to guard against its temptations. As they grow in experience the hope is that often enough they will make the best call for their child, enabling him to have the security he needs, the freedom to develop and a confident understanding of how to be in the world.

Parish ministry is not the same as mothering. There are inherent differences. Yet the likenesses can provide insights into what it feels like to be doing parish ministry. Like mothers, clergy are organizers, carers, comforters and at times admonishers. They provide spiritual food to feed the souls they are responsible for. They do 'housework', caring for the physical spaces which provide home for the faithful and welcome for the stranger. They are teachers, sounding boards and keepers of boundaries. They are companions on the journey, fellow travellers on the road, listening to and telling stories, using their knowledge to integrate these stories with God's continuing care for his people. They make plans, implement strategies, yet they know that these may be upset, disorganized and constantly redrawn to allow for the reality of other people's needs and other people's insights. Parish priests need to accept that this is an inexact science – more a creative art form. Thus they need virtues rather than formulas. It is a practice to be lived out with integrity, as they respond suitably in myriad different encounters.

What holds the practice together, what integrates it, is the motivation to care. The priest has accepted the responsibility to care for these people and this place. Like a mother, she makes plans because she cares. She 'tidies up' and does the necessary chores because she cares for these people. She teaches, challenges, sets boundaries and allows people to try things out, because she wants them to grow up and flourish. She longs for people to find comfort in their faith, freedom in their dependence on God and confidence in using their God-given gifts.

Clergy, like mothers, learn that they cannot get everything right. They learn that they need the help and collaboration of others. They need continual conversations to help them reflect on their practice, honing their understanding and skills as they glean insights from others. They need to learn how to forgive and be forgiven, to accept that sometimes trial and error is the right way of moving forward. They need to be authentic and trustworthy so that they can be relied on. It is about developing an appropriate character, cultivating the virtues which shape good practice – virtues such as humility, to guard against the temptations to dominate others or abnegate the responsibility they have been entrusted with, and resilient hopefulness, to keep on going when it is hard to define successful outcomes and others do not behave in ways that you had assumed they would.

Clergy need to trust God, to trust others and to be trustworthy themselves.

Ruddick reminds her readers that to name a virtue is not to possess it but to be clearer about the temptations which it guards against. Temptations often look like easier routes to the end goal, shortcuts that avoid the long and winding paths. For clergy the temptations of ministry are manifold. It can be tempting to try and minimize conflict by limiting discussion and questioning. Thus a priest might over-emphasize her expertise, making it hard for other opinions to be heard, or keep everything a bit bland so that no one gets upset, failing to talk about the difficult issues or admit where the answers are unclear. It is tempting to be validated by the neediness of others, so priests can behave in ways that make others dependent on them, caring over-intrusively, micro-managing every project and undermining those who do things differently. It can be tempting to be liked by all, and this might lead to a failure to challenge bad or inappropriate behaviour in others or to lose one's own authenticity and prophetic edge.

It can also be tempting to believe that the latest initiative, project or programme is going to answer all the issues and turn this church into a successful place. This can lead to a fixation on the programme rather than the people. The wrong measures of success and inappropriate models can mean that effort and energy are used in the wrong places and real gifts and moments of success pass unseen and uncelebrated. An unrealistic cheeriness can stifle critical advice and constantly promote unachievable goals with consequent feelings of failure. On the other hand it can be tempting to despair, to think that nothing will ever really work in this place with these people. Then a priest may blame herself, the place, the people, the diocese and even God for the problems of this church.

The reality is that there will be good days and bad days, bits of ministry that go well and bits that do not, and all of this can be unpredictable. When it goes well it can be hard to take the credit. Is this parish flourishing because I am a good priest or simply because it is full of people who get on and do things and the terrain is right for churchgoing? The answer is not clear. Winnicott says that children have either a good enough mother or a not good enough mother. This is also true for churches. Since the vicar is pivotal in a parish, a not good enough priest can unfortunately undermine the collective ministry of the congregation. She can unwittingly, or deliberately, stifle gifts, underfeed those who come for nourishment and limit growth. She may lack self-confidence and thus find it hard to listen to advice or to celebrate the success of others. She may be fearful, uninterested or too depressed to properly engage.

Yet with a good enough priest the growing confidence and maturity of those she cares for seems natural. The ministry flows out of the whole community and so much of what is done goes unremarked because it feels normal. Sometimes my children thank me for food cooked, washing done and advice given, but there is an underlying assumption that I am supposed to do this because that is what a mother does! So it is with good enough clergy. There will be moments when people recognize, acknowledge and affirm all the ordinary everyday things the priest is doing. Often, though, it will just be assumed that you are getting on with the job – nothing remarkable, just living out the calling.

The aim of this book has been to offer some ways of thinking and talking about the unremarkable everyday work of parish ministry. In doing so I want to affirm the discipline involved in loving and caring for congregations and parishes. It takes practice to learn to attend well to so many different people, to hold their needs in your head and heart. Being good enough does not happen without continued effort and commitment. There is plenty of juggling involved in managing the needs of communities, individuals and buildings. At times it can feel like being pulled in many directions, flitting from one thing to the next, without being able to truly focus properly. People and places change, so priests need to be ready to adapt, quick to read situations in context and to think and feel how to respond well. Like all things, with practice this juggling, thinking, feeling and responding becomes easier, and in time it almost seems instinctual. The more natural it feels, the harder it is to find the words to talk about it. Yet when we do not know how to talk about it, others may simply assume it takes no effort.

A few years ago we had a party for my son's eighteenth birthday. We gathered together friends and family who had in different ways been part of his life over the years. In my speech I said, 'They say it takes a village to raise a child, so thank you for being my village.' These people had collaborated in bringing up this child. Some had provided hands-on help, others through reflective chatting had helped me think through so many of the issues I had faced over the years. They had listened to my woes, my worries, my joys, my proud moments and my accounts of failure. These conversations had helped me hone my practice. My son, after a number of beers, thanked everyone for coming. Finally he thanked Mum and Dad with the words, 'After all, I am not perfect, but I am all right!'

As his parents we think he is more than all right. We delight in the semi-independent young man as he moves into his adult life. Some of the values and ways of behaving that we painstakingly modelled and taught have become unthinkingly part of his character. Other aspects are his own. There is evidence of boundaries challenged, ideas reinterpreted, mistakes made by us all and countless joys celebrated. Who I am is different because of the relationship we have had, the years of loving – at times frustrating – negotiation as we have adapted and changed over the years. Always in my mind has been the question: 'Is it well with the child?' 'Is there anything else I should do for him?' The heartaches have been plenty, the joys manifold and many. Has it all been a success? Well, as he said himself, 'not perfect, but all right,' which I think means it has been good enough.

I know that there are plenty of parishes that would, if asked, say the same kind of thanks to their parish priests. Thank you; we are not perfect but we are all right. You have not always got it right but you have got it right often enough and lovingly enough. You are human but, within your capacity, you have done your best to care for us as our priest. The ministry has been good enough, good enough for people to develop maturity, for people to feel at home and to feel able to bring others home. Good enough to provide the kind of sustaining care which does not smother but allows for the freedom to explore, to make mistakes and to be encouraged to move on. For those priests there will have been plenty of heartache but also manifold joys in the everyday wonder of seeing people and places flourish.

This book has tried to find some better ways of affirming this kind of ministry. It is not the end of a conversation but the start of one. I hope it encourages those engaged in parish ministry to find the words to celebrate what is being done, to name the virtues, resist the temptations and to find self-confidence that sets others free. The maternal metaphor is not the only one, nor even an exhaustive one. Yet it does offer a rich way of integrating the mundane and the mystical, the practical and spiritual, the being and doing, the highs and lows, the thinking and feeling, the joys and heartaches present in taking on the responsibility to care for real people in real places.

Notes

Introduction

1 See chapter 2 in Emma Percy, *Mothering as a Metaphor for Ministry*, Farnham: Ashgate, 2014.

2 Naomi Stadlen, *What Mothers Do: Especially when it looks like nothing*, London: Piatkus, 2004.

3 Sara Ruddick, *Maternal Thinking*, Boston, MA: Beacon Press, 1989.

1 A priest-in-charge

1 Anthony Russell, *The Clerical Profession*, London: SPCK, 1980.

2 Martyn Percy, *Clergy: The origin of species*, London: Continuum 2006.

3 Advertisement for Archdeacon of Dorking in *Church Times*, 12 July 2013.

4 This, of course, is under debate in terms of women priests. For those who maintain that a woman cannot be ordained because there is something essential in the masculinity of the priest, then a female priest simply is not a priest and therefore sacraments where she has presided are not true sacraments.

5 Percy, *Clergy*, p. 166.

6 Percy, *Clergy*, p. 166.

7 Beverly Gaventa, *Our Mother St Paul*, Louisville, KY: Westminster/John Knox Press, 2007, p. 6.

8 See chapter 2 in Emma Percy, *Mothering as a Metaphor for Ministry*, Farnham: Ashgate, 2014.

2 A relationship and an activity

1 Hannah Arendt, *The Human Condition*, Chicago, IL: University of Chicago Press, second edition, 1998; first published 1958.

2 Sara Ruddick, *Maternal Thinking*, Boston, MA: Beacon Press, 1989, p. 14.

3 Ruddick, *Maternal Thinking*, p. 104.

4 Donald Woods Winnicott, *The Maturation Processes and the Facilitating Environment*, London: Hogarth, 1965, pp. 145–6.

5 Donald Woods Winnicott, *The Child, the Family and the Outside World*, London: Pelican, 1964, p. 69.

6 Ruddick, *Maternal Thinking*, p. 72.

3 Playing the gift game

1 Iris Murdoch develops the idea of attention in *The Sovereignty of Good*, London: Routledge & Kegan Paul, 1970.

2 Sara Ruddick, *Maternal Thinking*, Boston, MA: Beacon Press, 1989, p. 120.

3 Ruddick, *Maternal Thinking*, p. 121.

4 Sue Gerhardt, *Why Love Matters: How affection shapes a baby's brain*, Hove: Gunner-Routledge, 2004, p. 197.

5 Congregational studies can help in thinking about telling congregational stories. See James Hopewell, *Congregation: Stories and structures*, Minneapolis, MN: Augsburg Fortress Press, 2006.

6 Ruddick, *Maternal Thinking*, p. 98.

4 Dependence and interdependence

1 Bonnie Miller-McLemore, *Also a Mother*, Nashville, TN: Abingdon Press, 1994, p. 184.

2 Jessica Benjamin, *The Bonds of Love: Psychoanalysis, feminism and the problem of domination*, New York, NY: Pantheon, 1990, p. 14.

3 N. T. Wright, *Virtue Reborn*, London: SPCK, 2010.

4 Celia Allison Hahn, *Growing in Authority, Relinquishing Control*, New York, NY: The Alban Institute, 1994, p. 22.

5 Hahn, *Growing in Authority*, p. 164.

6 Nel Noddings, *Caring: A feminine approach to ethics and moral education*, Berkeley, CA: University of California Press, 1984, pp. 69–71.

7 Brita Gill-Austern, 'Love understood as self-sacrifice and self-denial: what does it do to women?' in Jeanne Stevenson Moessner (ed.), *Through the Eyes of Women*, Minneapolis, MN: Augsburg Fortress Press, 1996, p. 312.

8 Beverly W. Harrison, 'The power of anger in the work of love: Christian ethics for women and other strangers' in C. S. Robb (ed.), *Making the Connections*, Boston, MA: Beacon Press, 1985, pp. 3–21.

9 Hannah Arendt, *The Human Condition*, Chicago, IL: University of Chicago Press, second edition, 1998, p. 201.

10 Hahn, *Growing in Authority*, p. 157.

5 Constantly interruptible

1 Lisa Baraitser, *Maternal Encounters: The ethics of interruption*, London: Routledge, 2009, see especially pp. 81–3.

2 Naomi Stadlen, *What Mothers Do: Especially when it looks like nothing*, London: Piatkus, 2004, pp. 33–4.

3 Baraitser, *Maternal Encounters*, pp. 146–50.

4 Nicholas Henshall, 'Best foot forward', *The Tablet*, 2 June 2012, p. 12.

5 Daphne de Marneffe, *Maternal Desire: On children, love and the inner life*, London: Virago, 2006, p. 40.
6 Stadlen, *What Mothers Do*, p. 68.
7 Stadlen, *What Mothers Do*, p. 60.

6 Weaning: the art of managing change

1 Bruce Reed, *The Dynamics of Worship*, London: Darton, Longman and Todd, 1978. Reed also founded the Grubb Institute, which ran many courses helping people to reflect on his ideas about systemic thinking and leading organizations.

7 The food is in the fridge

1 Sara Ruddick, *Maternal Thinking*, Boston, MA: Beacon Press, 1989, p. 87.
2 The Very Revd Michael Sadgrove, keynote address given at BIAPT conference, York University, 18 July 2013.
3 William Countryman, *Living on the Border*, Harrisburg, PA: Morehouse Publishing, 1999, p. 160.
4 Bruce Reed, *The Dynamics of Worship*, London: Darton, Longman and Todd, 1978, pp. 13–14.
5 Ruddick, *Maternal Thinking*, p. 87.

8 Living up to the calling – being good enough

1 Naomi Stadlen, *What Mothers Do: Especially when it looks like nothing*, London: Piatkus, 2004, pp. 18–19.
2 Daphne de Marneffe, *Maternal Desire: On children, love and the inner life*, London: Virago, 2006, p. 120.
3 Sara Ruddick, *Maternal Thinking*, Boston, MA: Beacon Press, 1989, p. 104.

Bibliography

Arendt, H. (1958; second edition 1998) *The Human Condition*, Chicago, IL: University of Chicago Press.

Baraitser, Lisa (2009) *Maternal Encounters: The ethics of interruption*, London: Routledge.

Benjamin, J. (1990) *The Bonds of Love: Psychoanalysis, feminism and the problem of domination*, New York, NY: Pantheon.

Countryman, W. L. (1999) *Living on the Border*, Harrisburg, PA: Morehouse Publishing.

De Marneffe, D. (2006) *Maternal Desire: On children, love and the inner life*, London: Virago.

Gaventa, B. R. (2007) *Our Mother St Paul*, Louisville, KY: Westminster/John Knox Press.

Gerhardt, S. (2004) *Why Love Matters: How affection shapes a baby's brain*, Hove: Brunner-Routledge.

Gill-Austern, B. (1996) 'Love understood as self-sacrifice and self-denial: what does it do to women?' in J. Stevenson Moessner (ed.), *Through the Eyes of Women*, Minneapolis, MN: Augsburg Fortress Press, pp. 304–21.

Hahn, C. A. (1994) *Growing in Authority, Relinquishing Control*, New York, NY: The Alban Institute.

Harrison, B. W. (1985) 'The power of anger in the work of love: Christian ethics for women and other strangers' in C. S. Robb (ed.), *Making the Connections*, Boston, MA: Beacon Press, pp. 3–21.

Kilby, K. (1997) *Karl Rahner*, London: Fount.

Miller-McLemore, B. J. (1994) *Also a Mother*, Nashville, TN: Abingdon Press.

Miller-McLemore, B. J. (2007) *In the Midst of Chaos: Caring for children as spiritual practice*, San Francisco, CA: Jossey-Bass.

Murdoch, I. (1970) *The Sovereignty of Good*, London: Routledge & Kegan Paul.

Noddings, N. (1984) *Caring: A feminine approach to ethics and moral education*, Berkeley, CA: University of California Press.

Noddings, N. (2002) *Starting at Home*, Berkeley, CA: University of California Press.

Percy, M. (2006) *Clergy: The Origin of Species*, London: Continuum.

Reed, B. (1978) *The Dynamics of Worship*, London: Darton Longman and Todd.

Ruddick, S. (1989) *Maternal Thinking*, Boston, MA: Beacon Press.

Russell, A. (1980) *The Clerical Profession*, London: SPCK.

Stadlen, N. (2004) *What Mothers Do: Especially when it looks like nothing*, London, Piatkus.

Winnicott, D. W. (1965) *The Maturational Process and the Facilitating Environment*, London: Hogarth.

Wright, N. T. (2010) *Virtue Reborn*, London: SPCK.

Index